Order from
TAN Books & Publishers
P. O. Box 424
Rockford, Illinois 61105

the
social
doctrine
of the
catholic
church

alba house
A DIVISION OF ST. PAUL PUBLICATIONS
Staten Island 14, New York

the social doctrine of the catholic church

THE MOST REVEREND EMILE GUERRY,
Archbishop of Cambrai

including the complete text of
MATER ET MAGISTRA

Second Printing, February, 1964

NIHIL OBSTAT
E. Hawrick
Censor Deputatus

IMPRIMATUR
✠Carolus Grant
Vic. Gen., Northantoniae

die 19a iunii 1961

Library of Congress Catalog Card Number 62-13995

Printed in the United States by Society of St. Paul
2187 Victory Boulevard, Staten Island 14, N. Y.

Contents

PART II

PART III

The Christian concept of the social economy can be
recognized by the following characteristics:

THIRD CHARACTERISTIC

AN ORGANIC ECONOMY 139

FOURTH CHARACTERISTIC

A DYNAMIC ECONOMY INSPIRED BY SOCIAL JUSTICE AND CHARITY 163

PART I

The Importance of the Social Teaching of the Church

Although Holy Church has the special task of sanctifying souls and of making them sharers of heavenly blessings, she is also solicitous for the requirements of men in their daily lives, not merely those relating to food and sustenance, but also to their comfort and advancement in various kinds of goods and in varying circumstances of time. Realizing all this, Holy Church implements the commands of her Founder, Christ.

—Mater et Magistra, 3-4

How many Catholics believe, in all good faith, that their Church's social teaching is a matter of choice, a sort of optional doctrine? This serious mistake is undoubtedly responsible for the lack of understanding, neglect and abandonment of the social doctrine of the Church in the recent past.

It is important to make quite clear, at the very outset, that a Catholic worthy of the name is obliged to follow the social teaching of his Church. The hierarchy is explicit on the point. Speaking of the social doctrine of the Church, Pope Pius XII declared in 1945: IT IS BINDING: NO ONE CAN IGNORE IT WITHOUT DANGER TO FAITH AND MORALS.[1] In 1947 he vigorously reaffirmed that this social teaching of the Church shows us the way to follow and that nothing, "no fear of loss of worldly goods or benefits, no fear of seeming opposed to modern civilization nor of appearing unpatriotic or lacking in social consciousness, can excuse true Christians for deviating, even by a single step from this path."[2]

In 1952, speaking to the Austrian Catholics and through them to all the faithful, the same pope exhorted them "to follow faithfully the clear line of Catholic Social Doctrine... without deviating to right or left. A deviation of only a few degrees can seem unimportant in the beginning. In the long

---

1 Pope Pius XII, Allocution to the Congress of Italian Catholic Action, April 29, 1945. See also Mater et Magistra, Paragraph 239. (Hereafter, references to Mater et Magistra shall be indicated as M.M., followed by the paragraph number.)
2 Different features, consciously or not, can be invoked: some by industrialists, others by militant workers or intellectuals.

run this deviation will lead to a dangerous separation from the right path." [3]

In France "The Pastoral Directory in Social Matters for the Use of the Clergy" adopted by the Plenary Assembly of the Hierarchy on April 27, 1954, lays down in Article 24, "the priest should never deviate from the social teaching of the Church."

In the exhortation, *Menti nostrae,* Pope Pius XII declares that "the damage caused by the two economic systems (capitalism and communism) should convince everyone, and priests in particular, that they should adhere and remain faithful to the social teaching of the Church."

The Plenary Assembly of the French Hierarchy declared in April, 1954 that "one of the gravest deficiencies of the present day is the underestimation or ignorance of the social teaching of the Church."

In *Mater et Magistra,* Pope John XXIII elaborates upon these points as follows:

> What the Catholic Church teaches and declares regarding the social life and relationships of men is beyond question for all time valid. . . .[4]
>
> Above all, we affirm that the social teaching proclaimed by the Catholic Church cannot be separated from her traditional teaching regarding man's life. Wherefore, it is our earnest wish that more and more attention be given to this branch of learning. . . .[5]
>
> But social norms of whatever kind are not only to be explained but also applied. This is especially true of

---

3 Pope Pius XII, Radio Message to Austrian Catholics, September 14, 1952.
4 M.M., 218
5 M.M., 222, 223

the Church's teaching on social matters, which has truth as its guide, justice as its end, and love as its driving force. We consider it, therefore, of the greatest importance that our sons, in addition to knowing these social norms, be reared according to them. . . .[6]

. . .it is not enough for men to be instructed, according to the teachings of the Church, on their obligation to act in a Christian manner in economic and social affairs. They must also be shown ways in which they can properly fulfill their duty in this regard. . . .[7]

Such warnings from popes and bishops impose a duty in conscience to know, study and propagate the social teaching of the Church. It is therefore of the greatest importance that we should know exactly what this teaching is. Unfortunately, there are misunderstandings and confusion on this point which must be cleared up, for they are largely responsible for the lamentable attitude of many Christians.

---

6 M.M., 226, 227
7 M.M., 230

I

WHAT IS THE SOCIAL TEACHING OF THE CHURCH?

The teaching of Christ joins, as it were, earth with heaven, in that it embraces the whole man, namely, his soul and body, intellect and will, and bids him to lift up his mind from the changing conditions of human existence to that heavenly country where he will one day enjoy unending happiness and peace.
—Mater et Magistra, 2

The social teaching of the Church is an embodiment of concepts (truths, principles and values) which the Church extracts from revelation and the natural law and adapts and applies to the social problems of our times in order to help, as she should, peoples and governments to organize a more human society in accordance with God's plan for the world. [8]

This definition of the social teaching of the Church sets out its sources, author, content, object and purpose.

I. THE SOURCES:

The concepts which make up the social teaching of the Church are drawn from revelation and the natural law.

---

8 M.M., 220

1. The *natural law* is inscribed by the Creator in man's very being, in his animal and rational nature, as understood by his intelligence. It is the expression in us of what our reason demands; it informs our conscience of what we should do to act in accordance with our rational nature, that we may not go against what is good and noble in man. It tells us to do good and avoid evil; good being what is in accordance with our rational nature—evil being what destroys its true development.

Chapter one will show the application which the popes have made of the natural law to the true concept of man in order to establish his fundamental rights and duties, his dignity and legitimate freedom.

In the second chapter we shall see how Pius XII and John XXIII in particular base their conception of the social economy on the natural law, placing man in the scope of the science of social economics. This science is not only the study of physical and mechanical phenomena but also of human acts—the acts of free men who ought to cooperate in the building of a social order in comformity with the order made known by God in the natural law and revelation. Certain economists erred by failing to appreciate the true nature of man and fell into a pitfall on this proposition. [9]

"The natural law is the foundation on which rests the social teaching of the Church," declared Pius XII. [10]

2. *Revelation.* Human reason has the power to discover and understand, through its own resources, the truths of the natural law and from these truths, to come to a true knowledge of a personal God. Nevertheless, because of the results

---

9 M.M., 175
10 Allocution to the members of the Congress of humanistic studies, Sept. 25, 1952

of original sin and the passions which always tend to cloud the intelligence and prevent man from seeing clearly and from judging correctly without self-deception, the First Vatican Council defined that, even for the truths of reason, revelation as well as the authentic teaching of the Church is morally necessary in the present state of the human race. Revelation confirms the natural law. It surpasses, expands, and deepens it.

Revelation is presented to man in two phases: the Old Testament and the New.

In the revelation of the Old Testament we find, besides the cultural and judicial laws, a moral law which is an expression of the natural law. The Decalogue sets out duties to God, rights and duties concerning the human person, the family, the neighbor. Except for the Third Commandment, which contains a positive divine command to reserve the Lord's Day for divine worship,[11] the commandments do not go beyond the resources of human reason. They are, therefore, binding as an expression of natural law but their authority is reinforced by the fact that they are a positive manifestation of the Divine will and because they are part of the great and free gift of God's Covenant.

On the social plane, a most important place must be accorded to the Prophets who denounced injustice, proclaimed the rights of the poor and lowly, and preached social and religious justice.

In the New Testament, Jesus Christ Himself said that He did not come to abolish the Old Law but to perfect it, particularly by the new commandment: "Love one another as

---

11 The third commandment defines, in a concrete manner, the precept of the natural law to consecrate time to the Lord. Cf. M.M., 249.

I have loved you." [12] The New Law is that of charity which invests all virtues, particularly justice, with the grace of the Holy Spirit. The Gospels contain a complete teaching on riches and poverty, the use of the fruits of the earth and the establishment of a human community in which all men partake of the world's goods, destined by God to be thus shared. [13]

But the double revelation, as consistently unfolded through the ages, consists more in God's great design for the salvation of mankind than in particular precepts on one virtue or another.

God calls man to share in the free gift of His Divine Life—man refuses the gift and falls into sin—God decides, in His infinite mercy, to save him. He stirs up His chosen people, molds them and guides them by His Word. He speaks through His patriarchs and prophets who foretell the Messiah, Redeemer of His people. He speaks finally through His Son, Whom He sends into the world to save all men. Jesus Christ, the Incarnate Word, redeems humanity by His message of truth, His life, death and resurrection. He founds the Church which He makes His social Body, animated by His Spirit. As head of this Body He leads His people through mankind's social life and history so that they may bring together all men in unity and thus form the Whole Christ by the growth of this Body in charity. This is the plan for salvation the Church has reflected in its tradition and written into its dogma: Jesus Christ, the Son of God, is Mediator between God and men, the only Savior; and the Church is

---

12 The revelation of the New Testament takes up the precept of charity, extending it to all men and all nations and teaching that it is realized in Christ as model and source of this love.

13 M.M., 157, 158

messenger of the Truth, guardian of the moral law, the means of salvation, teacher of mankind through its different activities here on earth.

The Fathers of the Church applied this far-reaching plan of salvation to the social problems of their time in a very daring and vigorous moral doctrine on the use of wealth and the distribution of the fruits of the earth. It is the same Divine plan for mankind which today inspires the Church's intervention in the economic and social field. It is understood that the Church's social teaching derives its meaning from the wide perspective of God's plan for salvation. It is obvious, in reason and faith, that it must bind the Church's children.

II. THE AUTHOR (*the efficient cause*).

It is necessary to make a most important clarification here to dispel many misunderstandings and ambiguities about the social teaching of the Church. Many active Christians still refuse to subscribe to the social teaching of the Church because certain schools of thought have quoted this teaching to justify positions or courses with which the former did not agree.

Pius XII has made a clear distinction in this matter:

"This institution (the Gregorian University) has undertaken the teaching of the social doctrine of the Church whose principal points are contained in the documents of the Holy See, that is to say, in the encyclicals, allocutions and papal letters. On this subject different social schools have appeared which have explained the pontifical documents and have developed and classified them. We think that they were right in so doing. But it was impossible to avoid that, in the application of principles and conclusions, these same schools should not move apart and fairly often differ among themselves. Also, in this context, what we said earlier about the teaching of the Catholic faith and theological schools must be remembered and care must be taken not to confuse the authentic doctrine of the Church with the different positions taken by each school; the two aspects should always be distinguished with great care." [14]

Thus, two aspects should be carefully separated: on the one hand, the authentic social doctrine of the Church; on the other, the application of principles and conclusions in which one can discern different theologians, sociologists, schools and movements.

The work, research, and positions of these Christian sociologists and these schools do not constitute the social teaching of the Church herself. Before the pronouncements of the teaching Church, they can play a very important part in preparing and making available vital documentation and information. After the publication of the pontifical documents, they seek to comment on their teaching and explain them. But neither the preliminary work nor the studies—no matter how great their intrinsic value, nor how authoritative their propounders—form the official social teaching of the Church.

The pope's comparison is very enlightening. A clear distinction must be made between the teaching of the Catholic faith by the Church on the one hand and, on the other hand, the different theological schools which are not in themselves the official interpreters of the social teaching of

---

14 Pius XII, Discourse for the Fourth Centenary of the Gregorian University in Rome, October 17, 1953.

the Church. The Church alone is the gateway to salvation and, under the protection and guidance of the Holy Spirit, the source of all truth. In consequence, the Church is the only proximate and universal guide to the true meaning of her social teaching.[15]

III. THE CONTENT OF THE CHURCH'S SOCIAL TEACHING:

We have defined the social teaching of the Church as an ensemble of concepts made up of truths, principles and values.

—the truths are what one has to believe and know (moral and religious truths);

—the principles are what one has to do, put into practice (code of moral behavior);

—the values are what one has to respect, defend, and cherish (fundamental human rights).

These are concepts drawn from the natural law and revelation. The Church adapts and applies them to the social problems which arise in the changing circumstances of economic and social life.

Revelation brought a Christian concept of man, his origin, nature, dignity and destiny—a Christian concept of the world, of history, of social life and of the human community—a Christian concept of work, of the realities of life,

---

15 As we shall see later, Christians must apply themselves, under their own responsibility, to political, economic and social analyses and draw their conclusions with a view to action. The social teaching of the Church is not a ready—made program which has only to be applied. Christians still have to work out a program of action which, while it refers to this doctrine, will imply ideas and applications which are the complete responsibilities of the laity.

of love, of the family, etc. The social teaching of the Church is the application of these Christian concepts to the review of present socio-economic structures and to the building of a more truly human, social, and economic order.[16]

Whenever the Church speaks through her social teaching she does so in the name of truth and of principles which are *sub specie aeternitatis* and in the light of the divine law,[17] irrespective of whether it is a question of faith or morals, that is, of the conduct of the social man and of his way of life. If the Church speaks, she does so to protect and safeguard those supreme values [18] of the dignity of man and the eternal salvation of souls.

But the action of the Church as guardian of the deposit of faith and the moral law can appear under different aspects. Sometimes she *teaches* these principles and ideas directly, sometimes she *defends* and protects these values by her judgments on erroneous theories (liberalism, communism, nazism) or the economic structures which threaten them, (technocracy, state totalitarianism); at other times she proposes the concrete *application* of these principles (vocational organizations) and herself furthers their application as circumstances and place require. It is important to study the documents very carefully in order to distinguish in them absolute truths to direct our lives, and their pastoral application made by the Church—the latter requiring careful judgment.

---

16 M.M., 6
17 Pius XII, Radio Message to the World, December 24, 1951.
18 Pius XII, Message to Austrian Catholics, September 14, 1952: "The Church will fight with all her forces where the supreme values are at stake: the dignity of man and the eternal salvation of souls."

IV. OBJECT AND PURPOSE OF THE CHURCH'S SOCIAL TEACHING:

The essential purpose of the Church's social teaching is the advancement of the Kingdom of God through human relations and temporal realities for the salvation of men. In this way she wishes to fulfil her spiritual mission to unite all men in God and among themselves. This of course causes her to condemn whatever operates against the attainment of this goal and to support whatever furthers it. She cannot remain indifferent as to whether or not men and nations are on good terms with each other. Essentially evangelical, the Church becomes, in addition, a civilizing influence.

But the Church also pursues a proximate objective. She cannot, by herself, build an earthly city nor organize a temporal society. She leaves this to governments and nations. But "Guardian, by the will and order of Christ of the natural and supernatural order, educator of mankind, Mother who cannot remain deaf to the anguished cries which her children of all classes of mankind send up to her," [19] the Church wants to help men build a more human, more just, more brotherly society which will be more in accordance with God's plan for man and the human community. The Church effects this in the course of her particular mission and by an educational method. In purely temporal affairs the Church does not take the place of the state nor of the civil sphere of authority in the building and running of the earthly city. She leaves them to their creative work, just as God committed creation to man who fulfils it by his work, his intelligence and his efforts. She never ceases to proclaim that she does not attempt to "lay down rules for the purely

---

19 Pius XII, Radio Message to the World, December 24, 1942

technical aspects of the social organization." [20] But she shows the road to be followed. She gives all the heritage and values of the Christian life so that each one can draw on them according to his own particular genius and his special needs in order "to set up a society worthy of man, raise it to a spiritual level, and provide true well-being." [21]

In his Christmas message of 1955, Pius XII declared that there are "false or restricted visions of the world and of life accepted by modern men" and these prevent men from going to the heart of things and from recognizing the foundation which gives meaning and harmony to human actions.

The pope, on the contrary, gave a wide and true vision in his messages to the faithful and to the entire world. The social teaching of the Church projects into the social and economic order this great vision of the world and of life: it affirms "the absolute order of beings and ends" [22] according to reason and the Christian faith.

---

20 Pius XII, Radio Message, June 1, 1941.
21 Pius XII, Radio Message, December 24, 1940: "Guardian and mistress of the principles of faith and morals, her only interest and desire is to give all nations, without exception, with her education and religious methods, the clear source of the heritage and values of the Christian life, so that each nation, according to its particular characteristics, makes use of the doctrines and ethico-religious features of Christianity in order to establish a worthily human society, which will be highly spiritual and a source of true well-being."
22 Pius XII, Radio Message, December 24, 1944.

II

WHY HAS THE CHURCH
A SOCIAL DOCTRINE?

To this Church, the pillar and mainstay of the truth, her most holy Founder has entrusted the double task of begetting sons unto herself, and of educating and governing those whom she begets, guiding with maternal providence the life both of individuals and of peoples. The lofty dignity of this life, she has always held in the highest respect and guarded with watchful care. —Mater et Magistra, 1

There are three primary reasons why the Church should have and teach a social doctrine. Each is closely bound up with the Church's mission.

First: As educator of man's conscience, the Church should lead each human being to his supernatural destiny through the realities of this life.

Second: As guardian of the moral law, the Church has the right and duty to denounce all attacks by economic and and social institutions against the moral law.

Third: As the Mystical Body, the Church has the mission of uniting all men in the unity and love of Christ.

I

As educator of man's conscience the Church should lead human beings to their supernatural destiny through the realities of this life. It is in everyday things, in family life and in working, economic and social affairs, that men find, or lose, their eternal salvation. How? By acting in accordance with or against the moral law as laid down in the commandments of God and in the Gospels.

In more concrete terms, it is in the conscientious fulfilment of their duties to God, the duties of their state in life (professional, political and social) that men are saved by the grace of Jesus Christ, that is, by practicing with the help of divine grace the natural and supernatural virtues which their station in life requires.

THE MISSION OF THE CHURCH

The Church, as teacher, helps men to recognize and fulfil their vocations and their destiny.[1] She molds their consciences to recognize the duties of their different spheres of human activity. She teaches them, in particular, that the question of salvation pervades their whole economic and social life.[2] She reveals the true value of human endeavor in the divine plan.[3] She also reveals the spiritual meaning of work,[4] of human love,[5] of married life,[6] of art, technology,[7]

---

1 M.M., 1
2 M.M., 214, 246, 247
3 M.M., 243, 244
4 M.M., 259. Pius XI in *Quadragesimo Anno:* "And so bodily labor, which was decreed by divine providence for the good of man's body and soul even after original sin, has too often been changed into an instrument of perversion: for dead matter leaves the factory ennobled and transformed whereas men are there corrupted and degraded."
5 M.M., 257
6 M.M., 193
7 M.M., 209

and all the activities of the human community.[8] She shows men that civilization needs redemption to rediscover its true meaning in accordance with God's plan. The world needs to be purified by Christ, the Redeemer, for it is no longer the world which God created. Sin has passed this way. And so the Church points out that civilization can tend either to the progress of mankind, or to its destruction.[9] The Church tries to make civilization serve true progress and help man to achieve his final end. Her mission is to be of service and not to dominate.

The first aim of the social teaching of the Church is therefore to help Christians fashion the world according to their faith. From this can be seen the light and strength of the faith for the building of the earthly City. The study of the dangers to faith set up by conditions of life and work will be dealt with later.

WORKING OUT THE SOCIAL DOCTRINE OF THE CHURCH

Certain transformations of special importance have caused the Church to develop her social doctrine so that she may fulfil her role as educator of man's conscience in this modern age.

First of all, the industrial revolution of the nineteenth century caused considerable upheaval in the life of the individual, and of the family, as well as in society generally. It upset traditional class relations. The Christian conscience was confronted with grave problems: How could the social injustice, which threw the mass of workers into undeserved misery, be righted? How could the crying inequality of the

---

8 M.M., 65
9 M.M., 210

distribution of worldly goods be redressed? Had the workers the right to organize themselves to protect their interests? Had the state the right to intervene with social legislation to protect the weakest? How should the doctrines of liberalism and socialism be viewed?

To all these questions the encyclical *Rerum Novarum* gave the Church's answers. From then on a complete Catholic social science grew from the teaching of the popes who successively replied to the problems of conscience posed by social evolution.

Furthermore, "socialization" of human life developed rapidly and the interdependence and solidarity between men, groups, professions and peoples quickly emerged. Ethics, which had become excessively individualistic through historical circumstances, now became *social* ethics. The Church has, by her teaching, faced up to these new problems, and brought to light the virtues of social justice and charity. She has sought to reconcile the claims of the individual with the common good and showed how, according to the plans of both nature and grace, man is at the same time individual and communal.

In *Mater et Magistra*, Pope John XXIII comments on this situation as follows:

> One of the principal characteristics of our time is the multiplication of social relationships, that is, a daily more complex interdependence of citizens, introducing into their lives and activities many and varied forms of association, recognized for the most part in private and even in public law. This tendency seemingly stems from a number of factors operative in the present era, among which are technical and

scientific progress, greater productive efficiency, and a higher standard of living among citizens. [10]

And again:

> We regard it as necessary that the various intermediary bodies and the numerous social undertakings wherein an expanded social structure primarily finds expression, be ruled by their own laws, and as the common good itself progresses, pursue this objective in a spirit of sincere concord among themselves. Nor is it less necessary that the above mentioned groups present the form and substance of a true community. *This they will do only if individual members are considered and treated as persons, and are encouraged to participate in the affairs of the group.*[11]

Finally, a new phenomenon appeared with the progress of civilization: a more acute consciousness on the part of governments and people, of the dignity of man and of his aspirations for a more human life and for greater well-being. There was also recognition for his rights and liberties and his participation in public life, as well as for society's duties towards the under-privileged and the politically and economically weak. The duty to share the world's goods more equitably among the underdeveloped peoples was acknowledged. Here again the social teaching of the Church guided each one towards his destiny by means of those problems confronting his conscience. The popes, and more particularly Pius XII and John XXIII, have taught a whole conception of man and his dignity, rights and duties as well as the proper use of freedom

---

10. M.M., 59
11. M.M., 65

and its responsibilities. They undertook the defense of the human person against all the forces which threatened to come between it and the fulfillment of its destiny. Could they have done more? The problem posed by scientific and technical advances and their repercussions on the rapid evolution of this world is an enormous one. It is all the more difficult because this evolution never ceases and is even accelerating in certain sectors, outrunning the rhythm of the analysis which economists, sociologists, and politicians steadily and laboriously pursue.

II

As guardian of the moral law, the Church cannot allow the social and economic order to violate that law, but rather, she serves to help this order correspond to God's plan.

Since man should attain his destiny through upright living in the temporal order, it is most important to realize that this temporal order (political, economic, social) does not itself constitute by its organization, institutions, structures and spirit, an obstacle to the supreme destiny of the human person and of mankind. There are, however, societies and milieux where it is difficult, if not impossible, to remain faithful to the moral law and to live a Christian life.

For some time now religious sociology has established, by a factual analysis, the deep and often determining influence wielded by social and economic conditions on the moral and social lives of men and their families. These include housing, transportation, leisure, means of communication (press, movies, radio, television), wages and working conditions, economic, political and social factors (like alcoholism and prostitution), natural groups, education and parental control (breaking up of family life).

As far back as 1931, Pius XI said that the conditions of economic and social life are such that a very large number of people find the greatest difficulty in carrying out that work which, alone, is necessary for their eternal salvation.[12]

More recently, John XXIII has pointed out that social and economic conditions must be so ordered as to allow men time for spiritual duties and bodily rest:

> It is the right of God, and within His power, to order that man put aside a day each week for proper and due worship of the divinity. He should direct his mind to heavenly things, setting aside daily business. He should explore the depths of his conscience in order to know how necessary and inviolable are his relations with God.
>
> In addition, it is right and necessary for man to cease for a time from labor, not merely to relax his body from daily hard work and likewise to refresh himself with decent recreation, but also to foster family unity, for this requires that all its members preserve a community of life and peaceful harmony.
>
> Accordingly, religion, moral teaching, and care of health in turn require that relaxation be had at regular times. The Catholic Church has decreed for many centuries that Christians observe this day of rest on Sunday, and that they be present on the same day at the Eucharistic Sacrifice because it renews the memory of the divine Redemption and at the same time imparts its fruits to the souls of men.
>
> But we note with deep sorrow, and we cannot but reprove the many who, though they perhaps do not

---

12. *Quadragesimo Anno*

deliberately despise this holy law, yet more and more frequently disregard it. Whence it is that our very dear workingmen almost necessarily suffer harm, both as to the salvation of their souls and to the health of their bodies.

And so, taking into account the needs of soul and body, we exhort, as it were, with the words of God Himself, all men, whether public officials or representatives of management and labor, that they observe this command of God Himself and of the Catholic Church, and judge in their souls that they have a responsibility to God and society in this regard. [13]

The strong pronouncement made by Pius XII on the disorder of the present economic society is also well known. "The Church cannot shut her eyes to the fact that the worker, in his effort to improve his condition, comes up against a whole system which, far from being in accord with his nature, is in contradiction to the order of God, and His purpose for the fruits of the earth." [14]

The same pontiff also affirmed the Church's right to have a social doctrine when he declared "incontestable ... the Church's competence in that sector of the social order which comes in contact with the moral law, to judge if the basis of given social organization is in conformity with the immutable order proclaimed by God in the natural law and in revelation." [15]

Because a materialistic age and a false philosophy have misunderstood the true meaning of man and of his nature—

---

13. M.M., 249-253
14. Christmas Allocution, 1942
15. Radio Messsage, Pentecost, 1941. The Pope adds: "On the form given to society, conforming or not to the divine laws, depends and permeates the good or evil of souls."

because the rights of workers have been violated by an excess of free enterprise and an unbridled desire for profit —because the economic regime has left innumerable worker's families without hope of justice, charity or humanity, in an "undeserved misery" according to Leo XIII, because the national and international political order has been falsified, the Church has worked out her social doctrine.

She intervenes as guardian of the moral law. But she also acts under the title of mother. As mother she loves her children and cannot accept any situation which would harm them.

As Pius XII said, "How could the Church, as a loving mother anxious for the good of her children, remain indifferent to the prospect of their dangers, stay silent or pretend not to see or understand the social conditions which, willingly or not, make difficult or practically impossible a Christian state conforming to the commandments of the Sovereign Lawgiver?" [16]

But it is not sufficient for the Church to state what is wrong and evil. She wants the temporal order to conform more to God's plan and to the dignity of man.[17] She demands "the setting up of an economic and social order which will be more in accordance with the plan and the means to rebuild an abundantly fruitful social structure." [18]

The broad outlines of the program were clearly set forth by Pius XII in his Christmas message of 1942:

> 1. Respect for the dignity of the human person and for his rights.

---

16. Radio Message, Pentecost, 1941
17. Pius XII, Radio Message, September 1, 1944
18. Pius XII, Radio Message of June 1, 1941

2. Internal unity of society and of the family.
3. Nobility of work with all its implications for social reforms for the working classes.
4. Far-reaching reconstruction of the juridical order for the security of man and the protection of his rights against all arbitrary human intervention.
5. A concept of the state at the service of society of man and of his destiny.

THE NATURAL AND SUPERNATURAL ORDER ESTABLISHED BY GOD

It is the duty of Christians to build a world according to the natural and supernatural order designed by God.[19]

God made a moral order for man's good. It is this order which reflects human nature and which God laid down as the basis of man's communal life in time and space. In his very first encyclical, *Summi Pontificatus,* Pius XII declared the unity of the human race. He declared that it is wonderful to contemplate the human race in the unity of its origin in God: "with the same God, the same Father of us all. Who is above all things, pervades all things and lives in all of us;" [20] in the unity of its nature composed, in all, of a body and a spiritual and immortal soul; in the unity of its immediate end and its mission in the world; in the unity of its habitation, the earth, to the fruits of which all men have a natural right and which can be used to sustain and develop life; in the unity of its supernatural end which is God Himself, to whom everything must progress in the unity of means to reach this end.[21]

---

19. M.M., 4, 215
20. Ephes., 4:6
21. Pius XII, *Summi Pontificatus,* October 20, 1939

There is a natural order, even if its form changes with historical and social developments. Its essential characteristics remain always the same: [22] first, the family and private ownership for man's personal security, then, local institutions and vocational groups as complements to his security and, finally, the State.

Christians should unite with all men of good will, even those not in the Church's fold, to defend and respect the natural order. We shall see further on how Pius XII demanded loyal and effective cooperation for the creation of an economic and social order more in line with the real needs of human nature. This cooperation is also necessary to obtain a more rational and equitable distribution of the world's resources. More than half of mankind suffer from a growing hunger and under-developed peoples have urgent and complex problems. The social teaching of the Church, far from opposing the active cooperation of all, positively encourages it to answer the crying needs of mankind.

Pope John XXIII goes a step further and points to cooperation on an international scale as a necessity for solving contemporary human problems.

Since the relationships between countries today are closer in every region of the world, by reason of science and technology, it is proper that peoples become more and more interdependent.

Accordingly, contemporary problems of moment—whether in the fields of science and technology, or of economic and social affairs, or of public administration, or of cultural advancement—these, because they may

---

22. Pius XII, Christmas Message, 1955

exceed the capacities of individual states, very often affect a number of nations and at times all the nations of the earth.

As a result, individual countries, although advanced in culture and civilization, in number and industry of citizens, in wealth, in geographical extent, are not able by themselves to resolve satisfactorily their basic problems. Accordingly, because states must on occasion complement or perfect one another, they really consult their own interests only when they take into account at the same time the interests of others. Hence, dire necessity warns commonwealths to cooperate among themselves and provide mutual assistance.[23]

But when Christians study the relationship between the natural and supernatural orders they should hold fast to the truth and avoid two conflicting errors.

The first error is to deny the truth of the natural order, to believe that this order has no intrinsic value, that human nature is inherently evil, to make the natural order depend on supernatural grace for its existence. There is a stability in the natural order because it is based on man, a spiritual being, whose nature is turned towards God. Pius XII said: "the Church has affirmed the value of that which is human and in accordance with nature; without hesitation she has sought it out and developed it. She does not admit that man is only corruption and sin before God. On the contrary, in her eyes, original sin did not intimately affect his qualities and powers and even left essentially intact the natural light of his intellligence and liberty."[24]

---

23. M.M., 200-202
24. Pius XII, Allocution to Congress of Humanistic Studies, September 25, 1949

The same Holy Father also acclaimed modern technical conquests. "The Church loves and favors human progress . . . all research and all discoveries of the forces of nature made by technical progress are only the search for and the discovery of the greatness, the wisdom and the harmonious design of God." [25]

Finally, in his Christmas message of 1955, Pius XII denounced both the error of the modern man who is lost in his pride of human power and his domination of nature [26] and the mistakes of those who shut themselves up in "a disdainful and despairing solitude, suggested by their fear and inability to participate in the life around them."

On the other hand, there is the serious error of looking on the natural order as complete and exclusive in itself.[27] The natural order must be left open to grace, to the supernatural life which perfects the human order according to the plan laid down by God and also to the life with God by divine adoption, which was brought by Christ to the world.

Man's misfortune today is that he sets himself up in his supposed self-sufficiency, revels in his technical and material progress and then misunderstands the limits of human nature. He forgets original sin and its results which have deprived man "not of his domination over the earth but of the guarantee that he can exercise that domination." [28] He ignores the true meaning of sin, which causes deep and wide disorder in the life of men and of society. He does not know that man can find stability and harmony only in Christ, the Redeemer. A great and unique event occurred in the history of mankind:

---

25. Pius XII, Radio Message, Christmas, 1953
26. M.M., 209, 244
27. M.M., 205
28. Pius XII, Christmas Message, 1955

the Incarnation of the Son of God. The truth and effect of
this historical fact should be appreciated by men.[29] Christians particularly ought to know that "the Son of God made
man is the only solid bastion of humanity, even in its social
and historical life, and that in taking on human nature, He
confirmed that nature as the basis and rule of the moral
order." [30]

It is to these sources, consecrated by the word of God
made man, that Christians should bring back modern society.
The source of their faith should equip Christians for the
ordering of public life and they have a perfect right to join
different institutions and organizations for this end.

In so doing there is no reason to suppose that they are
not being true to themselves. On the contrary, they have no
aim but to serve the common good in accordance with God's
will. They remain open to every good endeavor and to all
true progress. They work with those who, obedient to the
light of reason, can and should accept Christian teaching,
at least in so far as it is founded on the natural law.

Thus Christians should cooperate in the building of a
world according to the natural and supernatural order
designed by God.[31] The Church, in her social teaching, sets
forth the basic principles and evolution of this order. In
showing men how to save the world and how to restore the

---

29. "Henceforth mankind cannot repulse and forget the place and habitation of God
on earth with impunity, for in the economy of Providence, this is necessary for the
establishment of harmony between man and his possessions, and between these and
God. St. Paul, the Apostle, described the whole of this order in an admirable
synthesis: 'It is all for you, and for Christ, and Christ for God.' Whoever would
ignore God and Christ from these indestructible groupings and would forget the
Apostle's words on man's rights over material things, would bring about a vital
break in the Creator's plan." Pius XII, Christmas Message, 1955
30. Pius XII, Christmas Message, 1955 Cf. also M.M., 219
31. M.M., 259, 261

temporal, social and economic order in Christ she does not contradict human nature. On the contrary, she frees men and human society from their self-conceit and thus from the weaknesses of their own limitations. She helps them to recover their natural integrity and to bring the economic and social order back into God's plan. In this way she ensures true consistency and security because "They were all created through him and in him; he takes precedency of all, and in him all subsist" (Col. 1:17)—for as grace purifies man's nature and renders him more truly man, so the Church while respecting the state in its own order, creates the climate which furthers the true accomplishment by the state of its mission as a state.

III

As the Mystical Body of Christ, the Church has the mission of uniting all men in Christ.

Mankind treasures the memory of its unity which has been broken by sin. Man's history is a record of his progress towards unity despite appearances and notwithstanding upheavals, wars and strife. The story of this struggle towards unity is the real meaning of history.

This too, though on a higher level, is the mission of the Church.

To unite all men, in spite of all that divides them (race, class, language, mentality, civilization) in a single Body, loved by His divine Spirit; to unite them in the communion of His Life and charity so that they might partake in the unity of the divine nature and the life of the Blessed Trinity; this is the sublime design of Jesus Christ for mankind which He expressed in His prayer to His Father: "Father that they may be one in us. . . ."

It is in the Church that this reunion of men redeemed by Christ starts. But it is Christ the Head Who, in His Body, which is the Church, by His divine Spirit brings about this unity so that the body may grow in His charity until all men have come to make up the new man "to the completed growth of Christ" (Ephes. 4:13) as St. Paul said, the Total Christ.

This unity of all men in Christ in the context of history is the third basis of the social teaching of the Church. Through her social doctrine the Church teaches all men how they should prepare here and now to accomplish collectively the destiny of mankind through their thought and action in family, economic, social, national and international planes.[32]

This is also the reason why the Church's social teaching judges those movements which directly or indirectly oppose the fulfilment of God's loving plan for men. It is for this reason in particular that she condemned Nazism and Communism, just as she now denounces the dangers of excessive nationalism.

Finally, if the work of the popes on behalf of world peace is to be properly understood, it must be placed in the perspective of the Church's mission for the unification of mankind through all the disruptions of history.

"The consciousness of that mission of peace has always shown itself to be alive and active in the Church, particularly in her Visible Head, the Roman Pontiff," Pius XII said. In the same discourse he also made it plain that the Church's social action and teaching take on their true meaning in the perspective of the last end and final judgment: "If the Church

---

32. M. M., 200-202

speaks and passes judgment on present day problems it is in the clear knowledge that she thus anticipates, by virtue of the Holy Spirit, the sentence which will be confirmed and sanctioned at the end of time by her Lord and Leader, the Judge of the Universe." [33]

---

33. Radio Message to the World, December 24, 1951

III

REPLIES TO OPPOSITION

What the Catholic Church teaches and declares regarding the social life and relationships of men is beyond question for all time valid. —Mater et Magistra, 218

To many, the Church's social teaching is an anachronism. There are those who say, "The social teaching of the Church is out of date today. It was designed for a Christian epoch but society has become secular. Modern states organize their own political, economic and social affairs."

Contrary to what the objection supposes, the social teaching of the Church was worked out in the present epoch precisely to answer the social problems facing modern nations.

One historical fact which has not been sufficiently heeded is very clear. Who was among the first to recognize and respect the autonomy of the temporal order in its own sphere and to define the respective spheres of influence of the Church and the modern State? Surely it was Leo XIII in his encyclical, *Immortale Dei,* of 1885. Six years later in *Rerum Novarum* the same pope set forth the essentials of the social teaching in its historical context. It was thus proclaimed that the teaching was designed for the new age when modern society began to emerge.

Far from being old-fashioned, the most striking aspect of the Church's social teaching is, to the unprejudiced, its up-to-date quality. Through it the popes project the light of the natural law, of dogma and of the moral teaching of the Church into the social problems of the time.

We also hear it said that, while the social teaching of the Church advocates a Christian civilization, this concept is unthinkable in our secular age.

The expression "Christian civilization" is ambiguous. It can be understood in two ways—one in contradiction to the Church's social teaching and the other in its true sense.

It is wrong to assert that Christian civilization is identifiable with a particular civilization at a given time. On the contrary, the doctrine holds that Christianity is bound up with no one civilization, but that it transcends all. Furthermore, not even in the Middle Ages was any civilization or culture entitled to call itself exclusively Christian or Catholic. As Pius XII said: "No one dreams of returning to the Middle Ages."

There is a second and more correct sense in which a civilization inspired by Christianity and in which Christians put their faith into practice in its institutions and public life, can be called a Christian civilization. Now it is these very principles and ideals affecting the economic, family and social structures which the Church teaches her children in order to guide them.[1] Pius XII demanded that Christians should consider it their principal duty to bring back modern society, in its structures, to the origins consecrated by the

---

1. "In these matters it is of great importance that new offspring, in addition to being very carefully educated in human culture and in religion—which indeed is the right and duty of parents—should also show themselves very conscious of their duties in every action of life."—M.M., 195

Word made Flesh. If Christians ever neglect this duty laid upon them, leaving inert, as far as it depends on them, the law's force for the ordering of public life, they betray their God Who came visibly among us in the stable at Bethlehem.[2]

When we realize that God's plan for mankind is the return of the world to Him in Christ, it is easier to understand the sense in which the Holy Father can say that those Christians who refuse their mission to bring modern society to God, in Christ, betray Him.

That society is not "sacral," i.e., that the organization of temporal affairs is no longer made under the authority and in the framework of the Church, is an undisputed historical fact. The popes have declared that the temporal society is autonomous in its own sphere. But Christians cannot sit back and let society be dominated by materialism, paganism, or atheism which are contrary both to the highest destiny of man and the establishment of a true, lasting and universal civilization. Christians are not to dominate the world but to serve, love and improve it.

Secularism fears the Church's encroachment, and takes the stand: "We recognize that Christians have a duty. But can the modern, secular states avoid seeing a threat to their independence in the social teaching of the Church? Does not this teaching call for a domination of the world by Christ and does it not therefore constitute a new kind of imperialism?"

The answer is, of course, in the negative. The modern state has nothing to fear for its authority and the legitimate exercise of its power from the social doctrine of the Church. For this is the doctrine which affirmed the state's right and duty to protect the workers by social legislation in an age

---

2. Radio Message, Christmas, 1955

when economic liberalism opposed state intervention in the social sphere. This is the social doctrine which teaches that the common welfare is the finest mission of the state in the regulation of society and that the authority of the state must therefore be obeyed.

As to the Church's role in the welfare of human society, it is well to consider the forceful words of Pius XII [3] and to compare the Church's attitude with that of modern imperialism to see how different they are.

Modern imperialism expands over territories conquered by violence; it seeks to lay hand on the living elements of society and maintains its grip through external pressure.

The Church, on the contrary, proceeds quietly. She seeks first of all to win man. She tries to form the complete man from within and with his free cooperation. She prepares him for his responsibilities in society, she molds him in his capacity as a spouse, parent, worker, citizen, and member of the state. Indeed the state is the first to benefit from this educational work which helps it to carry out its own mission.

Many Christians oppose the Church's social teaching because they defend the secularism of the state, and it seems to them that this teaching does not recognize the state's secular character.

The expression "secularism of the state" must be clearly defined if freedom of conscience is not to be gravely compromised.

The secularism of the state can and should be the statement of its autonomy in its own sphere of the temporal order and in the exercise of its functions and services in the political, economic, administrative, judicial, military and educational

---

3. Discourse to the Consistory, February 20, 1946

spheres, etc. In this domain the state has nothing to fear from the Church's social teaching or action. Quite the contrary, as the popes have declared on innumerable occasions. We mentioned earlier that Leo XIII set forth this principle in the encyclical *Immortale Dei;* the French hierarchy developed it in a detailed declaration at the Assembly of Cardinals and Archbishops in March, 1945.

But in this same important declaration the French hierarchy differentiated between secularism in the correct sense and another meaning, i.e., a philosophical doctrine of secularism by which the state would impose secularism in men's minds in the schools, administration and public service to the point where God, His Gospel and His moral law would all be denied, and efforts made to present the Church as seeking to dominate modern society. This anti-religious concept must obviously be opposed by the Church in her social teaching, since it undermines freedom of conscience, the state's own mission and true secular character, as well as the rights of God, social peace and national unity. The state's refusal to acknowledge a superior, universal, moral code, founded on the natural law, leads directly to absolutism as Soviet Russia is now experiencing and as Hitler's Germany did experience. Peace is constantly imperilled by this absolute independence of state, which goes so far as to deny any international moral code and, by its aggravation of aggressive nationalism, provokes wars.

Finally, a third meaning is given to the term "state secularism". Superimposed upon it is the idea of absolute separation of state and religion, whereby the organization of the state, the courts and public authorities are supposed to ignore completely all religious activity, and thus the Church herself.

But the real meaning of the secular character of the state is quite different. The state cannot refuse to recognize the existence of religious authorities. It cannot ignore the fact of religion without denying the daily realities of life. It allows a place to religion, not only in its individual, but also in its institutional and social aspects.

The problem which arises is that of the demands of the public order. It is true that differences sometimes arise between Church and state on the meaning of public order, because the state holds that she has the right to define her own powers in this sphere.

But the social teaching of the Church can shed most useful light on this matter, particularly with regard to the common good and the role of the state. A state disposed to respect freedom of conscience would certainly be well advised, in its own interest, not to ignore the teaching of the Church.

One rather common view in opposition to the social teaching of the Church may be summed up as follows: The social teaching of the Church is limited in its application and can affect only Christians. But it is vitally necessary, if we are to build the earthly City, to have understanding and loyal cooperation between all men of good will on certain fundamental points acceptable to all. Let us look at the facts.

In his major messages during World War II, Pius XII made moving appeals to men of good will outside the Church for their loyal and effectual cooperation in order to create a better judicial order and "to create an economic and social order which would better correspond to the divine law and human dignity." [4]

---

4 Radio Message, September 1, 1944

In his address to the Catholics of the entire world, June 2, 1948, he declared: "They should not hestitate to join their efforts to those of men, who, while they are outside their ranks, are nevertheless in agreement with the social teaching of the Catholic Church. . . ."

On this question of working together with all men in social and economic affairs, John XXIII has stated that Catholics "should be prepared to join sincerely in doing whatever is naturally good or conducive to good." [5]

The popes themselves have shown how the social teaching of the Church has been welcomed by men far removed from the Church and has already deeply influenced them.

At the beginning of *Quadragesimo Anno*, Pius XI recalls the considerable repercussions of the encyclical *Rerum Novarum* in all sectors: it "began little by little to penetrate among those also who, being outside Catholic unity, do not recognize the authority of the Church and thus, Catholic principles of sociology gradually became part of the intellectual heritage of the whole human race. Thus, We rejoice that the eternal truths proclaimed so vigorously by Our illustrious predecessor are advanced and advocated, not merely in non-Catholic books and journals but frequently also in legislative assemblies and in courts of justice."

It is important to remember the public tribute paid to the Church's social teaching and to the encyclicals in international meetings and by eminent statesmen. For example, in his reports to the International Labor Office, Albert Thomas, one of the former leaders of French Socialism, never failed to pay tribute to the Church's social teaching and its influ-

---

5 M.M., 239

ence in .the world. In his report in 1928, the director of the International Labor Organization said: "The great movement brought forth by the Catholic Church in *Rerum Novarum* continues to bear fruit," and he cited documents and facts. In his report of 1929 he concluded his remarks on this point with: "Thus it would appear that the moral force of the Church can powerfully aid the work of social justice." On May 14, 1931, in a solemn assembly, before the delegates of fifty governments, M. Thomas Cortes paid official tribute on behalf of the I.L.O. to the encyclical *Rerum Novarum*: "In this assembly of working mankind we hear trade-unionists, politicians, and ministers of labor call on *Rerum Novarum* and, under the active inspiration of its principles, bring us their convinced cooperation. Thus the moral force of the Catholic Church and her spirit of conciliation can forcefully aid the work of international justice and good will."

History will one day show how peoples and heads of state were influenced by the powerful Christmas messages of Pius XII and also by his numerous allocutions addressed to representatives of different professions and nationalities. He thus started a direct method of teaching through personal contact with his listeners. His audiences saw reflected in his personal and paternal interest in their particular problems the Church's concern to guide all men through the errors and dangers which surround them.

Since the Church's social teaching is founded on revelation, it is sometimes held that those who do not believe in this revelation cannot accept the Church's teaching.

We said earlier that the Church's social teaching is founded on the natural law. Now this basis can unite all those who place their confidence in rational human nature. The social teaching of the Church appeals to straight reason.

It gives a concept of man which can be admired even by those furthest from the Church herself. It defends man's fundamental rights and personal worth. It calls for a human economy, the common good, social justice and brotherly love. How then can it fail to appeal to those who, anguished by the emptiness and futility of other teachings in the face of the overwhelming problems posed by man's own technical and economic progress, feel the need to unite with their fellows to save man and civilization?

Revelation brings a new light which surpasses but does not extinguish the light of reason. The life of grace embraces the life of nature to transfigure without destroying it. Revelation discloses man's supernatural destiny, God's divine plan for him and the means of his salvation. But revelation does not contradict the findings of reason and the natural law. It confirms them and guards them against error. To the natural motives for cooperating in the building of a social and economic order revelation adds others which are imperative for the Christian—motives of faith, of hope, and of love of God and neighbor. This is what Pius XII underlined in his message of September 1, 1944, when he appealed to collaborators and comrades in the struggle for the great work of reconstruction of a world shaken to its foundations and shattered in its very constitution. Speaking of the Christian readiness to work with others in a true spirit of brotherly cooperation, the Holy Father declared that "such a disposition surpasses simple obedience to the moral obligation of civic duties: it raises itself to the dignity of postulate of conscience, sustained and guided by the love of God and one's neighbor."

Another strong objection to the Church's social teaching is that it is too rigid in its principles and too vague in their application. It is held that, since the teaching of the Church is made up of unchangeable principles, these cannot apply to a life which is essentially fluid and a world which is continually changing. On the other hand, the principles are deemed too abstract, too remote, too indefinite and too static to give clear and constructive answers to the complex social life of our age.

Actually, the social teaching of the Church has the characteristic of being both firm in its essential principles and flexible in their application to the needs of each epoch.

John XXIII insists first that the social teaching of the Church can be applied: "... in no better way can they show this teaching to be correct and effective, than by demonstrating that present day social difficulties will yield to its application;" [6] and second, that it must be applied: "Social norms of whatever kind are not only to be explained but also applied. This is especially true of the Church's teaching on social matters, which has truth as its guide, justice as its end, and love as its driving force." [7]

Having stated that the principles contained in the social teaching of the Church can and must be applied, the Holy Father further insists that "what the Catholic Church teaches and declares regarding the social life and relationships of men is beyond question for all time valid." [8] Whatever form society takes, these principles should always guide Christians whose social life is inspired by their faith. "Moreover, the Church by divine right pertains to all nations. This is confirmed by the fact that she already is everywhere on earth

---

6 M.M., 225
7 M.M., 226
8 M.M., 218

and strives to embrace all peoples. Now, those peoples whom the Church has joined to Christ have always reaped some benefits, whether in economic affairs or in social organization, as history and contemporary events clearly record." [9]

Furthermore, Pius XII taught us that there is a natural order in society. This order must be sought and found among the mists of history, and then reconstituted.

> The fundamental, ultimate and ageless laws of society cannot be shattered by an intervention of the human spirit. They can be denied, ignored, scorned and defied but never abrogated. Undoubtedly conditions change with the passage of time. . . . In any case, through all changes and transformation the purpose of all social life remains the same, sacred and binding, i.e., the development of the personal attributes of man, made in the image of God. The obligation to realize these unchanging purposes rests on every member of the human family no matter what legislator or authority he obeys. [10]

Furthermore, the Church does not want to present men with ready-made solutions. She respects the developments of history, the differences among civilizations and nations, the state's proper sphere of action and individual or collective efforts to build the earthly city. But she requires lay Christians to demonstrate in their actions the principles she gives them.

To help them find technical solutions, the Church has

---

9 M.M., 178, 179
10 Message of December 24, 1942

adapted the applications of unchangeable principles to the changes of each era. In this way both immobility on the one hand and relativeness on the other are avoided. The firmness of the principles takes nothing away from the force and flexibility of their practical application to modern needs.

Speaking of the social teaching of the Church, Pius XII declared in 1945: "This doctrine, definitely fixed in its fundamental points, is sufficiently wide to be adapted and applied to the changing needs of time provided that this is not to the detriment of its lasting and immutable principles." [11]

John XXIII has clearly stated that the principles of Catholic social teaching "must not only be known and understood, but also applied to those systems and methods which the various situations of time or place either suggest or require."[12]

Some schools of sociological thought contend that the social teaching of the popes does not, properly speaking, constitute a doctrine in the same sense as the term is used to define Marxism, Liberalism, Fascism or the like. It would be more exact, they claim, to describe it as Christian requirements in social matters.

The doctrine begins with the principles and requirements which form the subject matter of the Church's teaching, but the elaboration of the doctrine no longer devolves on the Church but on everyone who wishes to organize society.

It is true that the word "doctrine" (in relation to the Church's social teaching) does not have the same meaning as when it applies to an economic system or a political party.

---

11 Allocution to Congress of Italian Catholic Action, April 29, 1945
12 M.M., 221

In the latter sense it means a technical program in an exclusively temporal sphere. This is precisely the role that the Church refuses to adopt, but leaves to the public and secular powers. The hierarchy adheres to the word "doctrine" primarily because to abandon the traditional term, "social doctrine," would rapidly involve the risk of abandoning the very idea of the Church's teaching in social matters. And so, little by little, people would become unaware of the Church's right to have and teach a social doctrine.

Furthermore, the term "doctrine" as used by the Church has a very precise meaning. Etymologically it means, in effect, a teaching (docere). Now the mission of teaching moral and religious truths was entrusted by Jesus Christ to His Church, i.e., to the pope and the bishops in communion with him. The Church received the mission to adapt and apply these principles to the social problems of each era.

The answer lies therefore, not in the rejection of the term "social doctrine" but rather in a clear explanation of the word itself as the Church defines it.

CONCLUSION OF PART I

The Church teaches the doctrine and shows its application to human problems. It is with this as inspiration that nations and leaders as well as lay Christians should themselves look for technical solutions for the organization of temporal society. We have already noticed how the popes have appealed to the enterprise, spirit, vision, and courage of Christians and all other men of good will. The Church's social doctrine is one of liberation, action, and progress.

A significant statement of Pius XII shows both the reasons for the Pope's intervention and the role that nations and statesmen must themselves play in the construction of a better social and economic order:

> For Our part, We have made it Our duty, even in the face of opposition, to warn nations and leaders that after such confusion as this they will have to build a social and economic order more adequate both to divine law and human dignity, thus closely uniting all the conditions necessary for true justice and the Christian principles which provide the sole guarantee for salvation, good, and peace for all.[13]

This is a wonderful definition of the Church's social teaching and of the benefits it can give to the world if the Christians who have confidence in their Church and fully believe in the mystery of the Redemption know how to understand its application, discover its meaning and help towards its extension, despite those who consider it old-fashioned, narrow, and useless.

Our further study will be divided into two parts. The social teaching of the Church brings to the world:

1. A concept of man;

2. A concept of social economy.

---

13 Letter to M. Charles Flory, July 14, 1945

PART II

A Concept of Man

*In our day, a very false opinion is popularized which
holds that the sense of religion implanted in men by
nature is to be regarded as something adventitious or
imaginary, and hence, is to be rooted completly from
the mind as altogether inconsistent with the spirit of
our age and the progress of civilization. Yet, this
inward proclivity of man to religion confirms the fact
that man himself was created by God, and irrevocably
tends to Him. Thus we read in Augustine:* THOU HAST
MADE US FOR THYSELF, O LORD, AND OUR HEARTS ARE
RESTLESS UNTIL THEY REST IN THEE.

—Mater et Magistra, 214

The concept of man which the social teaching of the
Church brings to the world is founded on three essential
principles:

 I The dignity of the human person;

 II The fundamental equality of men;

 III The inalienable rights of man who is the subject,
  not the object, of these rights.

We will study each of these three principles in turn,
and will indicate how the popes applied them.

I

THE DIGNITY OF THE HUMAN PERSON

Whatever the progress in technology and economic life, there can be neither justice nor peace in the world, so long as men fail to realize how great is their dignity; for they have been created by God and are His children.

—Mater et Magistra, 215

On February 4, 1956, Pius XII received in audience the delegates to an international conference on human relations in industry. Referring to the responsibilities of employers, he said, "Every man has an absolute and transcendent value because the Author of human nature gave him an immortal soul."

Setting out the ruling principles which should guide the social reconstruction of the world, Pius XII demanded (while World War II was still in progress) that everyone should "render to the human person the dignity conferred on it by God from its creation." [1]

According to the social teaching of the Church, society is at the service of the human person to respect his dignity and allow him to attain his end and his full human development. "Society is made for man and not man for society." [2]

---

1 Radio Message, December 24, 1942
2 Pius XI, *Divini Redemptoris*

Pius XI, who proclaimed this daring maxim, explains it in his encylical. It does not mean that society should be subordinate to the selfish use of the individual but that man is a social being by nature and can fully develop his attributes only in society, thanks to the help it provides for his physical, intellectual, moral, family and social life. In other words, man is a human person who will realize his full autonomy in communion with others and in cooperation with other members of society.

Agreement is possible with all those who, even though outside the Church, are determined to defend the fact of man's dignity against the dictatorship of totalitarian states.

But differences arise about the nature of that dignity. The Church has her own concept: she gives human dignity a fundamental and unshakable basis.

What gives man his dignity? It is the fact that he was created in the image of God. "The dignity of man is the dignity of the image of God," said Pius XII in his Christmas message of 1944. Open the Bible at the story of Creation: (Genesis 1:26). "God created man in his own image: he created him in the image of God."

What is the meaning of that stupendous truth revealed by God Himself in Sacred Scripture and inscribed by Him in man's nature?

Two texts of Pius XII help us to understand it: "Thus one can hope to see emerge more clearly the authentic image of man, master not only of things but, above all, of himself, and conscious of his transcending, individual and social destiny, and of his responsibilities as a creature made in God's likeness." [3]

---

3 Discourse to the Congress of European-American Associations, September 18, 1955

"Man is primarily a spirit created in the image of God, responsible for his actions and his destiny, capable of governing himself and thus finding his greatest dignity." [4]

Created in the image of God means at the outset that man is "master of things;" he dominates the things of creation and inferior beings (animals, plants, etc.) rather as God rules the world. God gave man the earth and a share of His divine government so that, depending on his Creator, man could fulfil the creation and the universe. This is the explicit teaching of the Bible.[5]

But why has man this power to dominate other created things? It is because he is free while lesser creatures are not. He is "master of himself," says the Holy Father in the texts which we study, and "'responsible for his actions and his destiny."

The root of this freedom and this responsibility is man's spirit, the immortal soul he has received from his Creator, his intelligence, reason which will enable him to think, to choose and to govern himself as a human being. "Man is a personal being, endowed with intelligence and free will; a being who has the final choice of what he will or will not do." [6] He is made in the image of God, a being supremely personal and absolutely free.

In the end, what gives man his human dignity is the fact that he is conscious of his overriding destiny and responsible for his actions and his destiny: it is the realization that he has been made in God's likeness to imitate God's perfection,

---

4 Replying to the Respects of the Diplomatic Corps, March 4, 1956
5 "God said, 'Let us make mankind in our image and likeness; and let them have dominion over the fish of the sea, the birds of the air, the cattle, over all the wild animals and every creature that crawls on the earth.'" Gen. 1:26
6 Pius XII, Allocution to the Sixth International Congress on Criminal Law, October 15, 1954.

His goodness, and His love and mercy for men. He must use his intelligence and will to discover the true significance of his destiny and his actions. He must lift himself up to God to participate, as God has ordained, as a brother of Jesus Christ and with Him and by Him, in life eternal, in the divine Life of God and of the Blessed Trinity. This is man's destiny!

> We urgently exhort all our sons in every part of the world, whether clergy or laity, that they fully understand how great is the nobility and dignity they derive from being joined to Christ as branches to the vine. [7]

"Man," says Pius XII, "is the image of God, One and threefold, himself also a person, brother of the man-God Jesus Christ and with Him and by Him the inheritor of eternal life; this is his true dignity." [8]

The basis of the dignity of the human person is therefore God Himself.[9] It is on Him it rests and He is the reason that it is impregnable. It depends on Him. Man's supreme dignity and true freedom is found in the realization and loving acceptance of his filial dependence. He thus freely pays homage in adoration, love and submission to the Divine Will.

If this dependence on God constitutes the greatness of man, it is because his dignity, based only on God, depends on none other than God. Man is not subject to earthly things, neither to progress, to the machine, to money nor to technical

---

7 M.M., 259

8 Allocution to Fiat employees, October 31, 1948

9 John XXIII speaks of "... the dignity with which man is endowed because he is created by God and because God has breathed into him a soul to His own image." M.M. 249

progress. It is religion and not the perfection of the organization or of the equipment which gives the worker his dignity.[10]

Modern man thinks he can do without God. "No folly seems more characteristic of our time," says John XXIII, "than the desire to establish a firm and meaningful temporal order, but without God, its necessary foundation. Likewise, some wish to proclaim the greatness of man, but with the source dried up from which such greatness flows and receives nourishment: that is, by impeding and, if it were possible, stopping the yearning of souls for God. But the turn of events in our times, whereby the hopes of many are shattered and not a few have come to grief, unquestionably confirm the words of Scripture: 'Unless the Lord build the house, they labor in vain who build it.'" [11]

Still, man rejects the divine basis of his dignity. For him the supreme being is not God, but man himself. As a result we have "The drama of atheistic Communism" which has so deeply influenced history. "We are in the process of proving by experiment that where there is no God neither is there man ... in truth, there is no longer man because there is nothing which surpassess man." [12]

APPLICATION OF THE PRINCIPLE

Perhaps there are those who think principles are undoubtedly noble and desirable things but that they cannot be put into practice. As an example, and a complete reply,

---

10 Pius XII—"Neither work alone nor the most perfect organization nor the most powerful equipment are capable of forming and ensuring the dignity of the worker. Only religion and all that is ennobled and sanctified can do this."—Allocution to Fiat employees, October 31, 1948.

11 M.M., 217

12 Father de Lubac, *Le Drame de l'Humanisme Athee*, p. 62

let us look at some of the applications to which Leo XIII himself put this principle of human dignity in his encyclical, *Rerum Novarum.*

> No one may violate with impunity this dignity of man that God Himself treats with great respect.

There is a striking contrast between God's respect for human dignity and the attitude of too many human beings towards their subordinates. It will be noted that the prohibition is explicit and universal: "No one may violate. . . ." If this rule were applied wherever authority is exercised, in all public bodies, in factories and mines, workshops and offices, and also in the family, towards employees and servants, it is certain that there would be a new atmosphere throughout the country. Many of those who bear the heavy responsibility of authority still do not realize that the most important thing for the servant, the agricultural or industrial workers, the employee, or the client is to be respected as a human person. This principle has been applied also on the group level by John XXIII who points out that the true form of a community can be achieved "only if individual members are considered and treated as human persons. . . ." [13]

Leo XIII continues: ". . . As to the rich and the employers, they must never treat the worker as a slave; in him they must respect the dignity of a man, enhanced by the dignity of a Christian. . . . It is shameful and inhuman to use men as mere instruments of providing lucre and of reckoning their value only in terms of the strength of their arms."

---

13 M.M., 65

It is difficult to imagine today the shock these forceful words of the Head of the Church produced over seventy years ago. It was the formal condemnation of a practice only too common at the time. Leo XIII here lays down a moral rule of conduct valid for all time.

> It is forbidden for masters to impose work on their subordinates which is beyond their capacity or unsuitable for their age or sex.

From this vigorous prohibition, which still remains relevant, as well as from the important efforts of political and trade-union movements, has sprung legislation to control the work of women and children and to limit the number of working hours.

Pius XI, in *Quadragesimo Anno*, noted the influence of *Rerum Novarum* on labor legislation. "From this persevering effort a new right was born, which the previous century had completely ignored. This was an assurance for workers of the respect they are entitled to as of right, as men and as Christians; e.g., their health and well-being, family, accommodation, workshops, wages, insurance against occupational risks, in a word, everything which affects the condition of the workers and particularly of women and children is the subject of this protective legislation."

Pius XII explicitly states that the doctrine and social standpoint of Leo XIII are founded on the principle of man's supreme destiny. "There is no doubt that the statement of man's supreme destiny constitutes the heart of the teaching of Leo XIII on labor questions." [14]

---

14 Rerum Novarum.

In the same trend, Pius XII, speaking to the workers at the Fiat plant of Turin, explained that the social reforms the Church advocates are inspired by the principle of the dignity of the human person: "If the Church, in her social teaching, always insists on due regard for the innate dignity of man; if she demands a just wage for the worker in his contract of employment; if she exacts adequate assistance for him in his spiritual and material needs, surely the reason is that the worker is a human being and his capacity for work should not therefore be considered as mere merchandise!"

II

FUNDAMENTAL EQUALITY OF MEN

If Christian precepts prevail...they will understand and feel that all men are the children of the common Father, that is of God; that all have the same end, which is God Himself, who alone can make either men or angels absolutely and perfectly happy; that all and each are redeemed by Jesus Christ, and raised to the dignity of children of God, and are thus united in brotherly ties both with each other and with Jesus Christ...
                                                    —Rerum Novarum

To the first principle of the dignity of the human person, the Church relates a second on the fundamental equality of men. Because every human being, no matter how lowly his social position, possesses this dignity there exists between men an innate equality.

On the subject of this dignity Leo XIII said: "From this point of view all men are equal; there is no difference between rich and poor, masters and servants, rulers and subjects." [1]

THE PRINCIPLE

Notwithstanding differences of age, position or physical, intellectual or moral attributes there exists a fundamental

---

1 Rerum Novarum

equality in nature. All men share one and the same origin in the order of nature: they possess the same human nature, the dignity of which is stated and defended by the Church.

Above and beyond this natural equality, which everyone, even the unbeliever, can acknowledge, the Church teaches that Christians share a higher equality in the supernatural order. They share the same faith and hope, the same destiny, the same Baptism, the same Eucharist—all have been ransomed by Christ and admitted to the same table—all are members of one and the same body. And it is the same Spirit which united this body in a single love. All have been adopted by the same Father in Heaven. All are called by the Son to become sons in a single family, the family of the children of God, which is the Church.

RESULTS AND PRACTICAL CONSEQUENCES OF THIS PRINCIPLE

Unbelievers, and perhaps some nominal Christians, are doubtless tempted to neglect the second, supernatural aspect of the equality of men because this domain is strange to them. They should make the effort to see the practical results of such a principle on a Christian who is determined to live his faith and to love Christ sincerely. This principle, rather than that of natural equality, is the basis of the brotherhood of men.

Saint Paul himself pointed out the practical consequences in decisive terms: "There is neither Jew nor Greek; there is neither slave nor freeman; there is neither male nor female. For you are all one in Christ Jesus." [2] Thus, there

---

2 Gal. 3:28

is an innate equality beyond all distinctions of race, nationality, position and sex. "In one Spirit we were all baptized into one body, whether Jews or Gentiles, whether slaves or free; and we were all given to drink of one spirit." [3] The innate equality of all men in Christ transcends secondary and artificial differences which set men against each other and also the natural differences between them.

The practical effect of this principle can be verified by the history of the early Christian communities. "Now the multitude of the believers were of one heart and one soul, and not one of them said that anything he possessed was his own, but they had all things in common." [4] Slavery could no longer be maintained in the face of this principle. The early Christians, applying the principle, shared all that they had, as religious orders and congregations do today, without distinctions of class, position or family background.

On the social plane, Leo XIII drew from these two first principles important consequences for the behavior of masters toward their servants: "It was ordained that masters should recognize the human dignity of their servants and treat them accordingly; not to consider servants as having a different nature from their masters' but, on the contrary, the same one; both have, in effect, the same religion and serve the same God." [5]

These are the same principles that the popes call on to establish better human relations between employers and workers, masters and subordinates. Pius XII said that the

---

3 I Cor. 12:13
4 Acts 4:32
5 Encyclical, *In plurimis*

equal human dignity of all which results entirely from the transcendental end common to all inspires them.[6] And again: "For the Church, all men are equal in dignity before God; they ought therefore to be equal also in the free or necessary relationships which unite them." [7]

Going beyond the framework of labor relations, he judges the great weaknesses of the social order in the light of these same principles. "The great weakness of the social order is that it is neither deeply Christian nor truly human but merely material and economic and that it does not rely on that which should be its basis and the solid foundation of its unity, i.e., the character common to men by nature and that of sons of God by divine adoption." [8]

The principle of the fundamental equality of men and the text of Saint Paul (neither Jews nor Greeks) condemn the racial segregation of certain countries today as well as the Nazi thesis of the superiority of the Aryan race. In this context it is useful to re-read the encyclical of Pius XI which condemns, in Nazism particularly, "the error of speaking of a national God, a national religion" which claim to imprison God, Creator of the universe, King and Law-giver of all nations, "within the frontiers of a single people, in the narrow confines of a community of the blood of a single race." [9]

To sum up, Pius XII called for "the recognition of the equality of all in the inviolability of personal rights." [10]

---

6 Allocution to the Christian Association of Italian Workers, May 14, 1953
7 Allocution to the International Congress on Human Relations in Industry, February 4, 1956
8 Pius XII, Allocution to members of the Christian Union of the leaders of Italian Industry, January 31, 1952
9 Pius XI, *Mit Brennender Sorge*
10 Christmas Message, 1949

NATURAL AND SOCIAL INEQUALITIES CONTRASTED
WITH THE PRINCIPLE OF THE EQUALITY OF MEN

It is a fact that inequalities exist beween men which seem to be in complete contradiction to the principle of innate equality. These inequalities come from different causes and are of varying importance. For the sake of clarity we will divide them into different categories.

There are, first of all, individual inequalities; human beings are born with differences of sex, health, physique, intelligence and talents.

Other inequalities spring from diversity of functions called for by the organization of society. Every nation must have men to fill public office and others to carry on the different professions necessary or useful for the common good, and these callings require different aptitudes and qualities.

There is also the inequality of condition, in the pos session of intellectual advantages, fortune and social position which arises from a difference of temperament or talents. Gifted men often succeed in obtaining high positions although they started in very modest circumstances. But, there are also those who succeed more because of inherited wealth and family influence than because of merit.

In the fourth category can be grouped the inequalities which are the result of the sins of individuals; unscrupulous and inhuman profiteers, who get on by every means, lawful and unlawful.

Finally, apart from inequalities created by individuals, there are inequalities arising from the disorder of society and the unfair distribution of the wealth of the world.

What is the Church's teaching on these inequalities?

Faced with the inequalities springing from nature, the Church tries to discover God's design.

As far as the inequalities of the sexes is concerned, the Church's social teaching is very full and lays down the exact sense in which it exists. She affirms the fundamental rights of women as being equal to those of men as far as their personal dignity is concerned: "in their personal dignity, as children of God, man and woman are absolutely equal" [11] ... "as far as personality is concerned they are entitled to equal honor, dignity, worth and respect." [12] The Church was the principal emancipator of woman from her degrading and unnatural slavery.

But it is the natural order itself which obliges us to recognize the natural diversity of gifts, character and temperaments in man and woman. "Certain (of these) are proper only to man and others only to woman, or they are unequally distributed, some being more developed in man and others in woman, because nature has given each a different sphere of activity and a distinct role to play." [13] The particular characteristics which distinguish the sexes have repercussions in family and community life. It is not possible to reverse this natural order "without nature herself always intervening to re-establish it." [14] And speaking of the awakening of nature thus thwarted, Pius XII states: "it remains to be seen if a readjustment (or reform) of the present social structure will not be brought about some day." [15]

---

11 Pius XII, Allocution to Italian women, October 21, 1945
12 Pius XII, Allocution to young ladies, members of Catholic Action, April 24, 1943
13 ibid.
14 Pius XII, Allocution to Italian women, October 21, 1945
15 Pius XII, Allocution to young ladies, members of Catholic Action, April 24, 1953.

Even though, in general, nothing can be done about the other inequalities of the first category, the Church's social doctrine repeats the great principle of respect of the human person, no matter what its weaknesses or its disabilities of childhood or old age. We know with what solicitude the Church surrounds children, the sick, the poor and the old and sets up social institutions to help, support and protect them.

The inequalities of the second category, arising from differences in functions and callings in society, are recognized by the Church as useful and good, once justice and charity are respected. They are in themselves a good thing from the point of view of society.

"This inequality operates for the benefit of all, individuals and society alike. Social life requires various qualities and different duties in its organization." [16]

These inequalities arising from different duties are not themselves an insurmountable obstacle to harmony in society. "In a people worthy of the name, all inequalities which spring, not from mere caprice, but from the very nature of things: i.e., inequalities of culture, of possessions, and of social position (without prejudice, naturally, to justice and mutual charity) are no obstacle to a true community spirit and brotherly love." [17]

The organic concept of society, borrowed from Saint Paul's image of the body—the body whose unity implies the diversity of functions for the individual and common good—

The pope drew a complete program of thought and action from these principles, the texts of which appear in *The Woman in the Modern World*, published by St. Paul Editions, Boston.

16 Leo XIII, *Rerum Novarum*
17 Pius XII, Message of December 24, 1944

explains, in the Church's social doctrine, the importance and usefulness she sees in the diversity of tasks. Discovering their need of each other, men are led to help and love each other and to collaborate for the common good of society.

Faced with inequalities of the third category—culture, possessions and standard of living—the Church offers a positive program which tends to diminish them progressively. It does so first of all by practical respect for everybody's fundamental rights, particularly the "right to sustain and develop corporal, intellectual, and moral life" (Pius XII), the right of every citizen to "a certain level of intellectual, moral, and physical culture" (Pius XI in *Divini illius Magistri*), and by insisting that the right to possess and use private property, "including that pertaining to goods devoted to productive enterprises, is permanently valid" (John XXIII in *Mater et Magistra*). It does so by the operation of the doctrine of the common good and of the demands of social justice and charity, and ultimately, by the application of this doctrine on the universal distribution of worldly goods. "It is not enough, then, to assert that man has from nature the right of privately possessing goods as his own, including those of a productive character, unless, at the same time, a continuing effort is made to *spread* this right through all ranks of the citizenry." [18]

Inequalities of the fourth category—fruits of men's sin and malice—are severely condemned by the social doctrine of the Church. Pius XI denounced these "profiteers, more or less numerous, who know, thanks to the power of money and organization, how to gain a privileged position over others." [19]

---

18 M.M., 113
19 *Quadragesimo Anno*

John XXIII has spoken very strongly about the need for justice in economic and social life: "For the great majority of mankind, work is the only source from which the means of livelihood are drawn. Hence, its remuneration is not to be thought of in terms of merchandise, but rather *according to the laws of justice and equity*. Unless this is done, justice is violated in labor agreements, even though they are entered into freely on both sides." [20] And again: "One may not take as the ultimate criteria in economic life the interests of individuals or organized groups, nor unregulated competition, nor excessive power on the part of the wealthy, nor the vain honor of the nation or its desire for domination, nor anything of this sort. Rather, *it is necessary that economic undertakings be governed by justice and charity as the principal laws of social life*." [21]

Already in his encyclical, *In Plurimis*, Leo XIII had described the disastrous effects of sin on the brotherly community of men: "All evils derive from original sin and notably that monstrous perversity by which there have been men who, forgetting their common origin with their brothers, instead of practicing good will and mutual respect, have listened only to their passions and begun to consider other men as being their inferiors and to treat them, in consequence, as animals born to the yoke." [22]

Finally, inequalities of the fifth category pose problems of the wrongful distribution of wealth. There are few subjects which have received more attention from the popes. They

---

20 M.M., 18
21 M.M., 38, 39
22 Leo XIII, *In Plurimis*, May 5, 1888

have all passed judgment on social inequalities due to present disorders of society and the economic system.

At the beginning of *Rerum Novarum* Leo XIII noted "the enormous fortunes of some few individuals, and the utter poverty of the masses."

Forty years afterwards Pius XI forcefully declared that "the immense number of proletarians [23] on the one hand, and the enormous wealth of the very rich on the other, are an unanswerable argument that the material goods so abundantly produced in this age of industrialism are far from rightly distributed and equitably shared among the various classes of men." [24]

Pius XII came back time and time again to this problem which preoccupied him. He drew attention to the growing number of workers who come up against wealthy interests which, under cover of their remoteness, succeed in totally neglecting their social duty and make it almost impossible for the worker to have anything for himself. [25]

The late pope said that "a more just distribution of wealth is, and remains, a main point of the program of Catholic social doctrine." [26] That there should be, within certain limits, an unequal division of the goods of the earth in the natural course of things is a fact neither economically nor socially abnormal. "But," continued the pope, "the Church opposes the accumulation of this wealth in the hands of a comparatively small number of very rich men while great classes are condemned to pauperism and an economic condition unworthy of human beings."

---

23 Persons not owning property.
24 *Quadragesimo Anno*
25 Radio Message, September 1, 1944
26 Pius XII, Allocution to Italian Catholic Action, September 7, 1947

John XXIII warns that "vigilance should be exercised and effective steps taken that class differences arising from disparity of wealth not be increased, but lessened as far as possible. . . . The economic prosperity of any people is to be assessed not so much from the sum total of goods and wealth possessed as from the distribution of goods according to the norms of justice, so that everyone in the community can develop and perfect himself." [27] "It is especially appropriate that today, more than heretofore, widespread private ownership should prevail, since . . . the number of nations increases wherein the economic systems experience daily growth. Therefore, by prudent use of various devices already proven effective, it will not be difficult for the body politic to modify economic and social life so that the way is made easier for widespread private possession of such things as durable goods, homes, gardens, tools requisite for artisan enterprises and family-type farms, investments in enterprises of medium or large size. All of this has occurred satisfactorily in some nations with developed social and economic systems." [28]

We will see in the second part of this study the remedies prescribed by the Church to correct this economic and social disorder. It is sufficient to note here that the principal reason that the Church rises against this unjust inequality is the same principle of the fundamental equality of men. It is obvious how relevant this social doctrine is and what a great influence it must have on any analysis of the social state and the urgent reforms needed, particularly for the betterment of the general populace and the improvement of the workers' lot.

---

27 M.M., 73, 74
28 M.M., 115

THE INALIENABLE RIGHTS OF MAN

Man has a spiritual and immortal soul. He is a person, marvelously endowed by his Creator with gifts of body and mind.... By sanctifying grace he is raised to the dignity of a son of God.... In consequence he has been endowed by God with many and varied prerogatives: the right to life, to bodily integrity, to the necessary means of existence; the right to tend toward his ultimate goal in the path marked out for him by God; the right of association and the right to possess and use property.   —Pius XI, On Atheistic Communism.

MAN IS A SUBJECT AND NOT A MERE OBJECT

Man is not a mere object which can be disposed of like an inanimate agent or some sort of tool. But this is what in fact happens too often. "In many of the most important activities of his life he has been reduced to a mere object of society." [1] This error has been frequently denounced by Pius XII. Material goods are not the only object of political speculations between nations—man too is used, "man lowered in so many cases to the level of a piece of raw material."[2] The popes have condemned the liberal economy and Communist socialism in turn because both, for different reasons, looked

---

1 Pius XII, Christmas Message, 1952
2 Pius XII, Allocution to members of the Congress on International Exchange, March 7, 1948.

on man as an object at the service of the economy. Pius XII spoke out against systems which do not protect the personal dignity of workers and "make their productive capacity a mere object which 'society' can fully exploit at its pleasure and will."[3] Stressing the fact that society is for man, not man for society, John XXIII affirms that "individual men are necessarily the foundation, cause, and end of all social institutions."[4]

Man is not an object; he is a subject by right. This expression is often found in the writings of Pius XII. It calls for the recognition and practical respect of the dignity of the human person and his rights, in social relations, in the life of the national economy and before the law. Men should be "considered and treated, not as objects but as subjects of the social life, particularly in the state and national economy."[5]

In social relations between employers and workers and for the discussion of working agreements, the practical statement that man is the subject and not the object of social relations provides the essential aim of trade unions, which is "to protect the individual against impersonal business interests which do not accept their social responsibility."[6]

In dealing with the national economy, Pius XII calls on the same principle to defend the right and liberty of men, who feel themselves closely united because of the objective goal of the social economy, to organize themselves in such a way that "the social order of the economy, far from attacking their freedom in the choice of means adapted to this end, will

---

3 Allocution to employees of Fiat in Turin, October 31, 1948
4 M.M., 219
5 Christmas Message, 1950
6 Pius XII, Message of December 24, 1952

guarantee and protect it. This holds equally good for every kind of worker, whether self-employed or not, for with regard to the end of the social economy, every producing member is the subject and not the object of the economic life." [7] This rule explains an idea dear to Pius XII; all those who, in any capacity, are involved in the social economy have the right to make their voices heard in the organization of that economy. They should be able to contribute their suggestions, ideas, and experience to bring about desirable improvements, for they are free subjects, intelligent and active.

John XXIII warmly praises what has been accomplished along these lines by labor organizations: "And we wish to praise paternally those dear sons of ours who, imbued with Christian principles, give their special attention to other labor associations and those groups of workingmen that follow the laws of nature and respect the religious and moral liberty of individuals." [8]

Finally, if the science of law has justice and injustice for its object, "the subject to which these rules of law are directed is man, the human person." [9]

Likewise, in plans and laws, "Every plan or program should be inspired by the principle that man as subject, guardian and promoter of human values is more important than material things and the implications of technical progress." [10]

---

7 Allocution to members of the Congress on International Exchange, March 7, 1948
8 M.M., 102
9 Pius XII, Discourse to Italian Jurists, November 6, 1949
10 Pius XII, Message of December 24, 1952

THE FUNDAMENTAL RIGHTS OF MAN

"Man, as a person, possesses rights he holds from God, which should remain, in the face of society, immune from all attacks that tend to deny, abolish, or neglect them." [11] The Church thus defends the rights of man which are inscribed in human nature and come from God, the author of that nature. The Church protects the fundamental rights of man against attack from all quarters. "In her eyes these essential rights are so inviolable that no reason of state, no pretext of the common good can prevail against them. They are protected by an insurmountable barrier." [12]

In the same passage Pius XII shows the considerable effect this principle would have in the world if it were universally respected. "If this principle were respected, how many tragic catastrophes and menacing dangers would be averted! By itself, it could renew the social and political physiognomy of the earth."

THE FUNDAMENTAL RIGHTS OF THE HUMAN PERSON

Pius XII listed the fundamental rights of the human person.[13] We will consider in particular those which affect

---

11 Pius XI, Encyclical on Nazism
12 Pius XII, Allocution to members of the Congress on Humanistic Studies, September 25, 1949
13 Christmas Message, 1942. "The right to maintain and develop physical, intellectual, and moral life, and in particular the right to a religious training and education; the right to worship God, both in private and in public, including the right to engage in religious works of charity; the right, in principle, to marriage and to the attainment of the purpose of marriage, the right to wedded society and home life; the right to work as an indispensable means for the maintenance of family life; the right to the free choice of a state of life, and therefore of the priestly and religious state; the right to a use of material goods, subject to its duties and to its social limitations."

Some of these rights are, at present, violated in certain totalitarian states. In other documents the pope added political rights, like the right of association, the

the social problem directly: the right to the use of material goods and the right to work.

The right to material possessions

An objection is immediately raised. "A doctrine which defends the right of private property has no hope of appealing to the masses. Once it states this right it appears as the protector of owners and consolidates both the privileges of wealth and the social inequalities which flow from them."

We reply in the first place that, if properly understood, this doctrine, on the contrary, answers the deepest aspirations of the masses. How many working-class families long to have a place of their own with, perhaps, a little land and basic security? This doctrine is the positive sign of how a man can better himself and his family.

Second, when closely studied, it becomes clear that this is a very bold doctrine, for it implies in effect a complete transformation of the economic society. The right is affirmed for all, including the most wretched and poor. In effect it means the disappearance of the proletariat, that is, of those who have nothing and who live in complete insecurity.

Third, this reform, ensuring the respect for a certain right to private ownership, is so necessary that the Socialist International procaimed it in its statutes of 1951.[14] Even in Soviet Russia the last few years have seen an important evolution in the sector of the small private holding.[15]

---

right to juridical security, the right to publish the truth and the right to life itself, which are also frequently violated.

14 The Socialist International "recognizes that Socialist planning is compatible with the continuation of private ownership in certain important sectors, and particularly in small and medium sized enterprises."

15 See Chambre's *Le Marxisme en Union Sovietique*, Chapter III: Capitalist ownership

To sum up, the extension of the workers' holding of some private property is an important claim in the social teaching of the Church. "The dignity of the human person normally demands the right to the use of earthly goods as a natural foundation for a livelihood, and to that right corresponds the fundamental obligation to grant private property, as far as possible, to all." [16]

Now economists foresee a revolution, already begun, in the notion of respect and protection for the small holding which corresponds to the needs and work of the human person. "In both capitalist and collectivist regimes," writes Father Bigo,[17] "an evolution of primary importance is taking shape, which tends to recognize the right to a certain amount of private property."

On the basis of a criterion that is not only material but also human, the author distinguishes property of the first and property of the second degree, according to its relation to man's need and work. While the latter is more and more submitted to collective authority, the former, because it is linked to the needs of family life and personal work, is respected. It has been re-established and promoted: "an effort is made to extend it to new sections of the population so as to afford the individual at least his minimal living space." [18]

John XXIII emphasizes the need for greater distribution of private property: "It is not enough, then, to assert that

has been completely liquidated in the U.S.S.R. But alongside state and the communal ownership of the Kolkhozien, Russian law recognizes a personal ownership which covers individual consumer goods and things like gardens, homes and tools. The owner cannot use them to exploit the work of others, but the regime was forced to break its rigid principles to concede at least this measure of private ownership.

16 Pius XII, Christmas Message, 1942
17 Marxisme et Humanisme, p. 235
18 ibid. p. 275

man has from nature the right of privately possessing goods as his own, including those of productive character, unless, at the same time, *a continuing effort is made to spread the use of this right* through all ranks of the citizenry." [19]

Far from being out of date, the Church's social teaching has led the way on this point.

Principles of the Right of Ownership

The Church's social teaching on the right of ownership can be summed up in the following principles:

1) The resources of creation are destined for all, and the goods of the earth are meant to be shared.

2) There is a distinction between the right of ownership and use: while the owner can use goods for a legitimate end, such use is always subordinate to a moral law which is binding on the conscience of the owner.

3) "The vital function of private ownership must be respected and protected in its personal and social role." —Pius XI

4) The present system of ownership is not unchangeable.

1) *The resources of creation are destined for all,* and the goods of the earth are meant to be shared. All the natural fruits of the earth belong in common to the whole human race without distinction. God created them for all men and they are at the disposal of all according to the principles of justice and charity. They should serve for the

19 M. M., 113

good of all and to give better living conditions to those who have need of them.

The first and fundamental right, which concedes in principle the use of earthly goods to all, dominates and enlightens this whole doctrine of ownership. It is particularly bold and far-reaching, and implies applications that the popes themselves have mapped out in certain spheres.

On the international plane this principle is the basis of the brotherhood of nations in the use of the world's riches for the betterment of humanity. Pius XII denounced the imbalance between the creditor and debtor nations.[20] John XXIII calls this lack of balance "the most pressing question of our day." [21] He presents the problem in detail, calls for action, and praises what has already been done to better the situation.

The problem:

> Perhaps the most pressing question of our day concerns the relationship between economically advanced commonwealths and those that are in process of development. The former enjoy the conveniences of life; the latter experience dire poverty. Yet, today men are so intimately associated in all parts of the world that they feel, as it were, as if they are members of one and the same household. Therefore, the nations that enjoy a sufficiency and abundance of everything may not overlook the plight of other nations whose citizens experience such domestic problems that they are all but overcome by poverty and hunger, and are

---

20 Allocution to the members of International Labor Office, March 25, 1949
21 M.M., 157

not able to enjoy basic human rights. This is all the more so, inasmuch as countries each day seem to become more dependent on each other. Consequently, it is not easy for them to keep the peace advantageously if excessive imbalances exist in their economic and social conditions.[22]

It is appropriate to recall at this point that in a number of nations there exists a discrepancy between available agricultural land and the number of rural dwellers. Some nations experience a shortage of citizens, but have rich land resources; others have many citizens but an insufficiency of agricultural land.[23]

Action required:

It is evident that both the solidarity of the human race and the sense of brotherhood which accords with Christian principles require that some peoples lend others energetic help in many ways. Not merely would this result in a freer movement of goods, of capital, and of men, but it also would lessen imbalances between nations.[24]

Praise for what has been accomplished:

Furthermore, we note that Catholic citizens of the richer nations are making extensive efforts to ensure that aid given by their own countries to needy countries is directed increasingly toward economic and social progress. In this connection, it seems specially

---

22 ibid.
23 M.M., 153
24 M.M., 155

praiseworthy that appreciable aid in various forms is provided increasingly each year to young people from Africa and Asia, so that they may pursue literary and professional studies in the great universities of Europe and America. The same applies to the great care that has been taken in training for every responsibility of their office men prepared to go to less developed areas, there to carry out their profession and duties.[25]

There are irritating discrepancies in the standards of living of different peoples which the brotherhood of nations demands should disappear. In the name of the fundamental principle of the sharing by all in the goods of the earth, Pius XII condemned "the narrow calculations of egoists, tending to corner economic resources and the materials of common use so that nations less favored by nature remain outside." [26] A true application was also made by Pius XII to the sad problem of immigrants.[27] "As long as the earth offers, anywhere, the means of feeding a great multitude," a state, having received certain guarantees, cannot refuse without just and reasonable cause, access to its territories to strangers who are destitute. It is necessary to bring about "a better distribution of men on the face of the earth that God created and prepared for the use of all." [28]

Within a single nation, in the name of the same principle, the popes call on men to relate the distribution of the world's

25 M.M.,183. Cf. also 156
26 Christmas Message, 1951
27 Pius XII, Letter to Most Rev. McNicholas, Archbishop of Cincinnati, December 24, 1948
28 Pius XII, Radio Message, June 1, 1941

resources to the needs of the common good and the norms
of social justice.[29] If, as we have seen, they condemn the
excessive disproportion between the gross fortunes of a few
and the miserable lives of many, and if they call for a more
equitable distribution of wealth,it is in order that "the goods,
created by God for all men, should belong to all equitably." [30]

Thus the same principle is invoked for a wider distribution of private ownership. The popes have shown the link
between private ownership and the fundamental principle
that the world's goods are destined for all.[31] The extension
of ownership to all men would make it possible for all to
exercise their right to the use of material goods.[32] The right
of private ownership, which comes in second place, is a
means of realizing the primary and fundamental right.

2) *There is a distinction between the right of ownership and use.* The owner has a true right over his property.
It is a natural right, i.e., men receive this right from nature,
and thus from God in so far as human nature has been created
by God and is His work. It is therefore a requirement of a
human being who, because he is rational and free, can and
should wisely organize the use of goods necessary for his own
needs and those of his family, not only in the present but for
the future. This implies the right to possess goods. If a man
holds this right from nature it is not derived from the state.

---

29 Pius XI, *Quadragesimo Anno*

30 Pius XII, Letter Sertum Laetitiae, November 1, 1939. Cf. also M.M., 113

31 Pius XII, Message of June 1, 1941; John XXIII, loc. cit.

32 Pius XI, *Quadragesimo Anno*, "that by means of it (private ownership) the goods
which the Creator has destined for the whole human race may truly serve this
purpose. Now these ends cannot be secured, unless some definite and stable order
is maintained."

He can exercise it as much over consumer goods as over means of production. [33]

The Church's doctrine makes a distinction between this right of disposing of and administering goods, and the use to which they can be put by the owner. According to this doctrine the owner can use them freely for a legitimate purpose, which is in this case a community purpose. Their use is subordinate to a moral law which is binding on the conscience of the owner.

Ownership is not, as the civil law says, the right to enjoy and dispose of things absolutely freely, within the limit of the law which prevents damage to others. He who owns something is truly its master. But this master is not the absolute master of his property. He is not free to enjoy it egoistically, soley to satisfy his personal whim and for his exclusive benefit. In the use he makes of it he should, on his own responsibility, take into account the fact that the world's goods are intended for the benefit of all and for the use of all.

Since ownership springs from a personal right which the state itself should respect and protect, it is not a social function at the service of the state. But it has a social function; it is subordinate to the common good. It is a right which entails social obligations. The principle of riches was clearly stated by Saint Thomas: "Man should not consider his

---

33 M.M., 19. Also, Pius XII, Message of September 1, 1944. In this passage the pope affirms the right of ownership over the means of production as well as over consumer goods, against those systems which deny the principle and render it impossible in practice. But the pope did not intend by this to accept any concept of private ownership. Shortly afterwards, in the same text, he condemns as contrary to the natural law that form of capitalism which, founded on erroneous ideas, takes to itself an unlimited right of ownership without any reference to the common good.

material possessions as his own, but as common to all, so as to share them without hesitation when others are in need." (IIa, IIae, q.66, a.2)

This is a bold principle: riches are intended for the use of the community; they should be used to assist those in need. There is undoubtedly no chapter of the Church's social teaching which is less known. There are even Christians who do not know that their religion obliges them in conscience to examine the source of their income, the use they make of it, the investment of their capital and the way they use their property. They feel they have done their duty by giving a few pennies to a street-beggar or putting a few coins in the collection basket.[34]

The masses are under a misapprehension when they accuse the Church of condoning the materialism of money and of covering up the abuse of wealth by approval or silence.

The Church's social teaching distinguishes two cases.

First, when one has enough for the necessities and reasonable comforts of life, there is a duty to give, out of what is superfluous, to the poor.[35] The duty is one of Christian charity on which we will be judged at the Last Judgment, and it is not an optional concession or favor showing outstanding generosity.

Of course, it is difficult to pin down the idea of "superfluous." What is important is that we should be constantly aware of this point. Conscience should be tuned in to the moral law, which it can interpret with the help of the Holy

34 Father Bigo, *Richesse et evangile,* Revue de l'Action Populaire, March, 1956
35 Leo XIII, *Rerum Novarum*

Spirit, Whose love marks the new regime instituted by Christ. We can only hope that through the movements of the Catholic Action the laity themselves will provide some practical yard-stick to measure this question.

But the principle is clear: all that is necessary to bring up and provide for a family in decent comfort, in keeping with its social position, (keeping in mind the necessary reaction of Christians against paganizing and excessively expensive habits arising from the pressure to comply with popular fashions and standards), must first be put to one side.

Apart from all that is thus necessary, the whole of the residue should be placed at the disposal of those who are in need in the name of charity, (love of God and our neighbor). The Christian who does not do this does not love.

Under what forms should this residue be utilized? Particularly as gifts, the placing of money and investments.

The *gifts* could be to organizations and movements which work for the relief of poverty and the needs of the poor. There are many such to-day.

The *surplus money should be placed* in the light of the Church's teaching that worldly wealth is for the common good: [36] such money can be invested in undertakings useful to the community but the object is not solely one of profit. The Church has a tradition on this point in her historic attitude to usury.

Investments might be for setting up or developing an enterprise to give work to the unemployed and thus would

---

36 Pius XI, *Quadragesimo Anno,* "A man's surplus income is not left entirely to his own discretion."

37 Father Bayart, "La propriete capitaliste et la doctrine sociale de l'Eglise." (Melange de Science religieuse, May and November, 1955, Lille).

distribute the use of wealth for the benefit of all.[37] Always providing, says Pius XII, that such work should be directed to produce really useful goods ... always serving the community.[38] Here the policy which creates false needs, through clever publicity, for the sake of large returns, must be condemned. On the same subject, what can be said of investments abroad made without any regard to the harmonious development of the country and which, in fact, upset its proper social and economic balance?

Second: case of extreme necessity. When a man finds himself in a state of extreme necessity there is a duty in justice to give him the necessities of life. One has no right to refuse them to him or to prevent him from taking them. On the contrary, he ought to take whatever is immediately necessary for him.

An example of what we mean is the present-day case of the homeless and of families which live in inhuman conditions in overpopulated and insanitary dwellings. From this example one sees the actual meaning of the doctrine—the principle seemed remote and hypothetical. We are only beginning to see its practical implications. It is to be hoped that this social doctrine will begin to inspire our legislators to remedy, in the name of social justice, these disorders which are so obviously contrary to God's plan.

---

38 An important remark. St. Thomas explains why a law is recognized in all human necessities, which seems too strong to many: "That which belongs to human law should derogate the natural or divine law. Now, according to the natural order established by divine Providence, inferior beings are destined to provide for man's needs; their division and appropriation—the work of human law—cannot prevent them from providing the needs of man. This is why whatever surplus wealth is held by some is due, by natural law, to the sustenance of the poor." These and other texts show that social justice requires those who have surplus wealth to help those in need.

3) *"The vital function of private ownership must be respected and protected in its personal and social role."* Pius XII. Private ownership has a vital function; it should serve personal, family and social life.

Personal life. Private ownership develops initiative and encourages men to make provision for the future. It is a stimulus to work and to save. It ensures the respect of man's dignity and freedom. That is why Pius XII links it to the freedom "from dependence and economic serfdom irreconcilable with human rights. Whether this serfdom comes from power of private capital or from the State the effect is the same." [39] "Moreover, experience and history testify that where political regimes do not allow to private individuals the possession also of productive goods the exercise of human liberty is violated or completely destroyed in matters of primary importance." [40]

Family Life. Ownership is necessary for family life to ensure its stability, cohesion, unity and independence. Pius XII defended the right of ownership in the name of the liberty of a father to provide for his family and fulfil his duties towards it.[41] He demands, for the family, vital living space.

Social Life. Because—and this is a psychological statement of common sense and experience—man pays more attention to his own property than to that which does not belong to him, private ownership brings about better management of goods and society at large thus benefits. Furthermore, when it is exercised with the sense of its social function and the wise distribution of whatever is superfluous, it is the

---

39 Pope Pius XII, Christmas Message 1942.
40 Mater et Magistra, 109.
41 Pope Pius XII, Message of June 1st 1941.

means wished for by God whereby, as the first principle laid down, the goods of creation attain their universal destination, being put to the service of all according to an order of justice and charity.

4) *The present system of ownership is not unchangeable. It has undergone and will undergo futher developments.* There is fairly widespread opinion that the Church is bound to the present system of ownership. She is accused of not recognizing the developments that the forms of ownership can undergo.

The whole social teaching of the Church refutes this very criticism. The popes have lashed out against the weaknesses, anomalies and inequalities of the present system.

No. The Church is bound to no single system of ownership. The Church always defends the rights of the human person. She is as independent of all kinds of economic systems as she is of all political ones. Pius XI declared in Quadragesimo Anno: "History proves that ownership, like other elements of social life, is not absolutely rigid." The pope then listed the various forms that ownership has taken; primitive forms of savage peoples, patriarchal era, feudal, monarchical and the varied forms of the modern age.

CONCLUSIONS

1) *The social teaching of the Church bases the right to the use of material goods on the dignity of human person* for this dignity is superior to created things which have been placed by Providence at the disposal of all men. The extension of private ownership to all requires that the principle that material goods are destined for the use of all men should

be practised according to justice and charity, as respected in human conventions.

2) *This doctrine establishes a synthesis beween the personal and social role of ownership.* It calls on every Christian, and indeed on every man, to make this synthesis in his conscience and conduct. To sacrifice the first aspect is to fall into socialism or communism. Not to recognize the second is to return to liberalism and pagan concepts of ownership.

3) In the teaching of Pius XII a distinction between two forms of ownership emerges. On the one hand *personal and family ownership,* closely linked with the human person and, on the other, the larger forms of *capitalist ownership.* In both cases the pope maintained the principle. But he vigorously denounced the abuses of the second category. It was in this sense that he condemned capitalism as "contrary to the natural law." "Wherever capitalism is based on false ideas and assumes a limitless right over its own property, without admitting any subordination to the common good, the Church has always condemned it as contrary to the natural law." [42]

It is true that the rapid development of economic structures seems opposed to the practice of the doctrine of personal and family ownership. The nature of the small family holding poses problems difficult to solve. First is that of change of residence to which the working population is subject owing to the "shifting of labor." Enquiries and census returns have shown how frequently this can occur today. Then there is the fact that the small house and

---

42 Pope Pius XII, Radio Message, September 1st, 1944.

garden lead to an agglomeration of such a size that the collective cost (roads, water, gas, electricity, sewage, transport, etc.) cannot be met from municipal revenues. Finally, how can the small farmer stand up to the requirements and expense of the mechanization of agriculture?

All these facts are indisputable and raise complicated problems. But first, as we have seen, the popes agree that the Church cannot be bound to any one form of ownership. Their attitude with regard to developments in economic structure shows their independence in this sphere. Indeed it is here necessary to appeal to Christians "to find new forms of ownership which better correspond to the essential function of worldly goods, which is the flowering of human life in its individual and social aspects." [43]

On the other hand, in defending the right of ownership, the pope places the metaphysical and moral point of view before everything else; the blossoming of the human person and the conditions of his freedom, responsibility and personal initiative remain essential whatever systems or forms prevail. The picture of the little house and garden does not show all the forms which family ownership can take in certain countries.

Finally, if the principle is abandoned, it must be seen that collectivism, with its grave consequences and problems, becomes the dominating power.

THE RIGHT TO WORK

Popes Leo XIII and Pius XI both taught that work had a twofold character; it is both personal and necessary. Pius

---

43 Mgr. Tiberghien: "sens chretien et vie social" p. 133.

XII continued this teaching: [44] and completed it by developing a third characteristic: work is social.

First characteristic of work: it is personal.

The Principle: "It is personal" that is to say the worker's human person in all its aspects is involved in his work. A person's entire physical recourse, his faculties of intelligence, initiative, energy and will, together with his responsibilities as a man and head of a family, are involved. These, and his motives and attitude to work, should teach him the true meaning of work, which is: a means of earning his living so that he can lead a decent, human existence and raise and support a family. Work is the true expression of the human person.

The Application: The applications of this principle proper to the doctrine of the Church, but which, nevertheless, everyone can and should accept, have been set out by the popes.

First, on the *dignity of work*. Here again, the Church's social teaching is opposed both to Liberalism and Communism, to Liberalism which equates work to merchandise, to Communism, which considers work solely as a productive force at the service of the Socialist State.

Both errors fail to recoginze the personal character of work. They consider it as though it can be detached from the person of the worker, as though it were not inherent in his person. Socialism recognizes the dignity of work but it puts this dignity into the work done and not in the person who does it.

---

44 Pope Pius XII, Radio Message, June 1st, 1941: "It is personal because it is accomplished by uniquely human forces; it is necessary because without it the necessities of of life cannot by procured."

For the Church's social doctrine, on the contrary, the dignity of work comes from the dignity of the human person of the worker. It is a *human act*. (Father Villain in "Enseignement social de l'Eglise," Vol. II, p.62, says: "We are here at the antipodes of pure Socialist thought; for if man has dignity because he works his dignity is in his work and still more in the final product. We, on the contrary, say that it is man who gives work its dignity and the source of the dignity of human work is in man.")

In the second place, the principle has its repercussions on the *conditions of work*. Because work is inseparable from the person and cannot be considered solely under its utilitarian and material aspects, the popes have forcefully called for conditions of work which respect the personal character and dignity of the worker. These conditions should take into account the physical resources and limitations of man so that his body may not be crushed and his soul stifled: [45] Man must have time to relax and to observe the Sabbath. Allowance must be made for age, sex and health of the worker and for the hazards inseparable from human life.

Finally, this principle is binding on the *State* which intervenes more and more in questions of the remuneration for work and which now itself owns certain industries. It should respect the personal character of work, says Pius XII, "both in principle and, as far as possible, in practice." Neither should the State's Laws render impossible the other rights which the pope listed.[46]

---

45 Leo XIII, Rerum Novarum: "To exercise pressure upon the indigent and the destitute for the sake of gain, and to gather one's profit out of the need of another, is condemned by all laws human and divine."

46 Pope Pius XII, Radio Message, June 1st, 1941.

The second characteristic of work: *It is necessary* because it gives the worker the means of earning his living and providing for his family.

Principle: Every man has the duty, imposed by nature and his Creator, of preserving his existence which he holds from God. He has therefore the right—imposed by nature and not by society—of finding in his work the means of providing for himself and his children.

In this precise sense, we can speak of the right to work— the worker's natural right to accomplish his duty as a worker, "as the indispensable supporter of family life" (Pius XII). This does not mean, as some Socialists held in the 19th century, that every individual out of work has the right to demand employment from the State although, as we will see later, the State has the duty in certain cases to provide work. But it does mean that, in a well-organized society, every man has the right to find in his work whatever is necessary to live a human life.

Practical applications:

1) *For the remuneration of work; Wages*: The Church's social teaching has contributed greatly towards impressing on the public mind two essential ideas; the minimum living wage and the family wage.[47]

The Living Wage.

The idea of a living wage is bound up with the essential character of work. Leo XIII in *Rerum Novarum*, fighting

---

47 These two problems have caused years of discussion and study both on the part of theologians and sociologists.

against the insufficiency of wages, then widespread under the free-trade system, taught that there was a minimum below which a wage would be unjust. This minimum is what is necessary for the worker's subsistence. The pope's text is well known and had a great effect because he recalled the requirements of the moral law and justice: "Let the working-man and the employer make free agreements, and in partic-ular let them agree freely as to the wages; nevertheless, there underlies a dictate of natural justice more imperious and ancient than any bargain between man and man, namely *that wages ought not to be insufficient to support a frugal and well-behaved wage earner.* If through necessity or fear of a worse evil the working-man accepts harder conditions because an employer or contractor will afford no better, he is made the victim of force and injustice." A wage is not just merely because it has been agreed upon between employer and worker, for it can happen that the worker is not free to refuse because he must find work at any price. A wage is just if it is in conformity with the higher law of natural justice which recognizes the *vital necessity* that the worker's wage should enable him to live as a human person.

In Quadragesimo Anno, Pius XI completed this idea of a living wage. He considered three factors in the remuneration for work. The first was *the needs of the worker.* He must keep himself and his family at a level which allows of certain amount of leisure and ease and provides against natural risks of sickness and old age and occupational hazards. Then Pius XI also took into account the situation of business or industry and the requirements of the common good. He called on social and vocational organizations for a policy which would solve the problems of the living wage.

The social teaching of Pius XII is characterized by his

insistence on a *just wage*. He came back time and time again to this point. He makes it, together with a better distribution of the natural goods, one of "the two most pressing requirements in the social program of the Church." [48]

In the second place, the pope undertakes *the defense of the women workers and their wages*: "the Church has always sustained the principle that, for the same work, the same salary should be paid—and women should be paid the same as men for the same work." [49] The pope denounces the injustice which can be done to the woman worker by workers themselves.

In the third place, a just wage, according to the pope, is one which sustains the worker and *his family*. "It is that which ensures the existence of the family and which enables the parents to fulfil their natural right of raising a family which can be decently fed and clothed." [50] Pope John XXIII, in his Encyclical Mater et Magistra writes: "Wherefore, we judge it to be our duty to reaffirm once again that just as remuneration for work cannot be left entirely to unregulated competition, neither may it be decided arbitrarily at the will of the more powerful. Rather, in this matter, the norms of justice and equity should be strictly observed. This requires that workers receive a wage sufficient to lead a life worthy of man and to fulfil family responsibilities properly." [51]

---

48 Pope Pius XII, Radio Message, March 11th, 1951 to the Christian workers, technicians and managers of Spanish industry.

49 Pope Pius XII, Allocution to menbers of the 1st Italian Congress of Women Workers, August 15th, 1945: "It is both unjust and contrary to the common good that a woman's work should be used only because it is cheaper, with bad results, not only for the women, but also for the male worker who is thus exposed to unemployment."

50 Allocution to Italian workers, June 13th, 1943.

51 M. M., 71.

The family wage:

The idea of the family wage is always intrinsically linked with that of the living wage. The popes have laid down the principle. But they left professional and political men to find the technical solutions. Pius XI also paid tribute to those who found practical formulae, like that of family allowances, a system invented by a socially-minded Catholic, M. Romanet.

2) Because work is necessary and a living wage is vital the popes have called for a *proper organization of the people's work*.

The right and duty of building this organization belong to those who are most immediately concerned—employers and workers. One thus sees how organization on vocational lines can meet the pressing needs of the social economy according to the ideas of the popes.

In his message of December 24th, 1952, Pius XII declared: "When private enterprise remains apathetic or insufficient, the public powers are obliged to procure employment in every way possible in undertaking works of public utility and to facilitate those looking for work by setting up Councils or Labor Exchanges." Where private enterprise fails the State must intervene and help in the distribution of work according to the requirements of the common good. Has not the *fight against unemployment* become one of the gravest preoccupations of the modern State? But the State is now too small a unit in this field. The problem is an international one. Pope Pius XII showed a most courageous attitude (see his Allocution of June 3rd, 1950, to an International Congress of Social Studies in Fribourg) calling for a coalition of the entire world, a universal collaboration of men of all nations to find the solutions together. It is

not only a question of a better distribution of the total
sum of the physical resources of all the workers of the world
but of giving innumerable families sufficient scope to
develop as natural, moral, legal and economic units. One
can see how the Pope, here too, took the side of the family.

Third characteristic of work: it is social.

The idea is a noble one and is understood by militant
Christians. It gives meaning to their work and provides an
ideal for their social action.

The Church's social teaching considers work as the
means offered by God to men to co-operate in His work of
creation and build together an earthly kingdom.

Thus, Pope Pius XII considered work as a unifying factor
among men because of men's nature. It brings them together
and links them in the accomplishment of an even greater task,
that of procuring for society the goods and services which
are necessary or useful for it.[52] It serves humanity and draws
men nearer to God.

Furthermore, according to the Church's social teaching,
work should become the means of human betterment. It
tends to improve the moral and material well being of the
worker and to develop his personality. Alas, the reality is
usually far removed from this ideal. Work in factories, mines,
and work-shops too often degrades and brutalizes the human
person.

---

52 Pope Pius XII, "Work unites men for the service of the people in a common effort
   which tends to the perfection of one and all to the glory of the Creator and of the
   Redeemer." Allocution to farmers, November 16, 1946. Pope Pius XII, Letter
   to M. Charles Flory, July 19th, 1947. "In this sense, work is capable, by its very
   nature, of closely uniting men together."

Pius XI said "Contrary to the plans of Providence, work, which was destined, even after Original Sin to perfect man materially and morally tends in such conditions to deprave him. Matter comes out ennobled from the work-shop while men are degraded and corrupted there." [53]

Here again we see the extent of the requirements of the Church's social teaching and the great changes she wants men to bring about, so that society's organization can come near to God's plan. "It is the complete and complex structure of society which needs to be changed and bettered." [54]

The high moral value of work. In God's plan work should help man to glorify God and sanctify himself. Even in the technological era, the human person created by God and redeemed by Christ remains noble in himself and, as a result his creative force and work have a more lasting worth. Thus consolidated, human work also has a high moral value and mankind at work constitutes a society which not only produces things but glorifies God. Man can therefore consider his work as an instrument of his own sanctification for in working he perfects the image of God in himself.[55]

CONCLUSION OF PART II

This concept of man that the Church's social teaching brings to the modern world has certain characteristics that were underlined in the teachings and work of Pope Pius XII.

In the first place it is concerned with human interests. Far from teaching a cold and inhuman doctrine Pius XII described the sufferings and miseries of men in moving terms.

---

53 Quadragesimo Anno. Also M.M., 242.
54 Pope Pius XII, Allocution to Italian workers, June 13th, 1943.
55 Pope Pius XII, Christmas Message, 1955.

Industrial and agricultural workers, the unemployed and economically depressed, the banished, exiles and migrants; children who have been abandoned, "families in blackest misery," the old and the poor; the oppressed of all kinds, "all those who suffer affliction for any reason," the millions haunted by the possibility of famine and the under-nourished populations ... the pope thought of them all and spoke of each group particularly. He explained that the sad chorus came to him from all parts of the world and that the "sorrows and tears it revealed rent Our very heart." [56] This is the echo of Christ's cry of compassion and mercy which is prolonged to our own day by His Vicar on earth: "I have had pity on the crowd" . . . "My soul is sorrowful."

The pope did not consider an abstract man, a "homo economicus," but living beings of flesh and blood who work, toil and suffer. He saw people as human beings who loved, bore the responsibilities of a family, and had needs and aspirations which must be taken into account in the name of justice and charity.

We can apply to Pius XII the words which he applied to the Church, "Watching constantly over man, listening to his heart-beats she knows his worth and perceives his aspirations with a clear sighted intuition and that penetrating vision which can only come from the supernatural light of the Church's doctrine and the supernatural warmth of His divine love." [57] The same thought is expressed by Pope John XXIII, "Our heart is filled with profound sadness when we observe, as it were, with our eyes a wretched spectacle indeed—great masses of workers who, in not a few nations, and even in

---

56 Radio Message, December 24th, 1952.
57 Allocution to the Sacred College, February, 20th, 1946.

whole continents, receive too small a return from their labor. Hence, they and their families must live in conditions completely out of accord with human dignity." [58]

A second characteristic which cannot but strike those who too lightly accuse the Church of not rating man highly enough, *is its dynamic realism.* Man, wounded and weakened as he is by Original Sin, is reminded by the Church that he still retains [59] the light of his intelligence and freedom and that he can and must fight if he is to be faithful to his supernatural duties and the natural law, and that he has the grace of God to help him. Pope Pius XII constantly and confidently called on man's freedom, will, energy and sense of responsibility so that he might take his place in the national economy and play an active role there instead of passively leaving everything to the State. The pope required each man personally, and all men together, to participate in the formation of the new order. He proclaimed his "confidence in the sense of right and justice deeply anchored in the human person." [60] This is true realism, "which determines, with the same certitude, the dignity of man and his limitations; his capacity to excel, but also the reality of sin," Pius XII, Christmas message, 1956.

In addition, how can one fail to be moved by the dignity of the interventions of the pope as Head of the Church? He rose above the scramble of nations and all the powers of money, politics, governments, opinions and technical progress

---

58 M.M., 68.

59 "Original sin and its consequence have deprived man, not of his power over the earth, but of his security in the service of that power." Pope Pius XII, Christmas Message, 1956.

60 Pope Pius XII, Allocution to members of the International Institute for the unification of private law, May 20th, 1948

*to undertake the defense of man and call for the liberation
of the human person.* The pope defends man against the
perils which menace him; against the errors and systems
which belittle human nature and tend to drag man into the
trap of false liberty, or enslave him to the dictatorship of
a man or a State. He also defends man against the abuses of
economic systems, against the socialization of everything,
against the collective irresponsibility of impersonal owners
and the hold of technocracy and against all outside pressures.
The pope warns man against the ambivalence of scientific
progress and defends him in the spheres of medicine,
psychoanalysis and surgery, as in the application of juridical
sciences and the process of the law, including certain police
methods.

For, in the words of Pope Pius XII, "everything should
tend to the liberation of the human person. God has placed
the human person at the summit of the created universe,
making him the standard for everything in economics and
politics." [61]

All inventions, progress, economics and techniques
should be judged in relation to man. "The Church's role is
to establish here an order of values and to subordinate factors
of material progress to pure spiritual elements." [62]

Finally, this concept of man regards him *as he is.* All
branches of knowledge—history, geography, sociology, psy-
chology, law, the sciences and medicine—should be devoted
to the return to man, the discovery of man and the search
for the place which belongs to him. In the midst of laborious

---

61 Pope Pius XII, Letter of 14th July, 1945 to M. Charles Flory.
62 Reply of Pope Pius XII to the Respects of the Diplomatic Corps on his 80th
birthday. (March 4th, 1956).

efforts to get men to improve international relations and find a true peace, Pope Pius XII, in his Christmas Allocution of 1955, made an appeal which is a whole Program in itself: "to refind peace and *give back to man his place in the world.*"

How could such a doctrine, taught fearlessly and with unflagging perseverence, fail to have deep repercussions on the social economy? This is what we will study in Part Three.

PART III

The Christian Concept
of the Social Economy

*"The cardinal point of this teaching is that
individual men are necessarily the foundation, cause,
and end of all social institutions. We are referring to
human beings, insofar as they are social by nature,
and raised to an order of existence that transcends
and subdues nature. Beginning with this very basic
principle whereby the dignity of the human person is
affirmed and defended, Holy Church—especially
during the last century and with the assistance of
learned priests and laymen, specialists in the field—has
arrived at clear social teachings whereby the mutual
relationships of men are ordered."*

—Mater et Magistra 219-220.

The Church's social teaching gives our age a concept of social economy bound up with the Christian concept of man. There is a "Christian concept of social economy." [1] This third part will be devoted to its analysis. This concept shows us how, without intervening in the organization of the technical aspects of the running of society, the Church fulfils her mission in the spiritual, moral and social order. She does not abandon men to their task but brings them the irreplaceable help of her principles, knowledge and experience of humanity and the wisdom of her popes, so that the citizens of this earthly kingdom and their governments can themselves build a social order nearer to the needs of men and leading to peace.

The Christian concept of the social economy can be recognized by the following characteristics. It is:

1) a human economy;

2) an economy for the common good;

3) an organic economy;

4) a dynamic economy inspired by the principles of charity and social justice;

5) finally, an economy obedient *to the moral law*.

---

1 Pope Pius XII, to members of the World Congress of Chambers of Commerce, April 27th, 1950.

A HUMAN ECONOMY

According to Pope Pius XII, the most important social problem is that of the organization of a social economy which would be directed towards satisfying man's needs; an economy which would respect man's nature and dignity and provide the material conditions in which he can live as a man should.

There are several characteristic traits of such a human economy as described by the popes:

1) that it should be *at the service of man;*
2) that it should take into consideration *man's nature;*
3) that it should adjust itself to *man's fundamental needs;*
4) that it should aim at *man's improvement;*
5) that it should be *available to all men;*
6) that it should *fit man* and be *made to a human scale.*

1) *At man's service.*

The economy should respect, pursue and guarantee the *primacy* of man over all material things, whether wealth, production or technical progress. Man's proper place in society from which he has been debarred for too long must be restored to him.[2] It is possible to organize the economy without taking man into account, so that a nation is considered only according to the riches and material wealth it has amassed. Everything must be sacrificed to production in such a society. The concept of a human economy entails a radical change from the ideas of the eighteenth and nineteenth century economists who used only natural philosophy, or from the concept of the totalitarian states which reduce everything to mere mechanics.

Not that a human concept of society fails to recognize the great importance of every nation's productivity, for without sufficient production there cannot be enough to go round [3] and the well-being of the population is sacrificed. But "productivity is not an end in itself." [4]

Furthermore, there is disruption when "this productivity is effected by means of unrestrained competition and the unscrupulous use of wealth or by despotic oppression and exploitation of labor and its particular needs, for the profit of state." [5] The order which must be respected is that which puts man in the central place and puts economy at his service. The Church has consistently endeavored to have man considered more important than economic and technical advantages.[6] "If the organization and structure of economic life be such that the human dignity of workers is compro-

---

2 Pope Pius XII, "The great wretchedness of the social order is that it is neither deeply Christian nor *truly human,* but purely technical and economic." Allocution to members of the Christian Union of the leaders of Italian industry, January 31, 1952.
3 Pope Pius XII, Allocution to Sacred College, June 2nd, 1948.
4 Pope Pius XII, Discourse, February 4th, 1956, to representatives of business and trade unions.
5 Pope Pius XII, Allocution to the Sacred College, June 2nd, 1948.
6 Pope Pius XII, Radio Message, March 11th, 1951.

mised, or their sense of responsibility is weakened, or their freedom of action is removed, then we judge such an economic order to be unjust, even though it produces a vast amount of goods, whose distribution conforms to the norms of justice and equity." [7]

2) *A human economy which takes into consideration human nature and the whole man.*

Technology is subordinate to man and to the sum of the spiritual and material values which concern his nature and personal dignity.[8]

If man comes first it is because of the dignity of his human nature and person. The human economy is one which takes into account the complex nature, the living unity of body and soul, individuality and personality of the whole man, a spiritual and reasonable being, a free and social being, child of man and son of God.[9]

—of man, the *corporal being*, needing food, health, relaxation and rest.

—of man, the *spiritual and rational being,* called to a life of reason and intelligence. A being called also to a spiritual, moral and religious life so that he may not become a slave to his senses, whims, instincts, and passions but become "man" and realize his vocation as a human person—to recognize his dependence on God—finally, called to a life with God as His son. An

7 M. M. 83.

8 Pope Pius XII, Christmas Radio Message, 1953.

9 Pope Pius XII, "The Church has not kept a narrow concept of man because she knows the complexity of his nature and understands human nature better than others" (Allocution to the International Federation of Engineers, Oct. 9th, 1953).

economy which does not allow man to live this higher
life is not a human economy.

—of man, *the social being,* bound to other men by a law
of solidarity in the different societies where he lives
and which are at the service of the human person;
particularly the family, his vocation, different sectors
of life, the national and international community. A
human economy is one which takes these social factors
into account.

—of man, the *free being,* able to co-operate and unite
with other men in the choice of means to guide the
social economy to its true end.[10] A being free from
centralized control of his economic and social life by
rigid and mechanical formulae which, because they
are so authoritarian and centralized, ignore all local
and regional differences and do not sufficiently associ-
ate the members of the national community in the construction of the "City." All large scale plans are useful
and necessary in so far as they serve man.

3) A human economy is one which "should adjust
itself to *man's fundamental needs.*" [11]

In his message of December 24th, 1952, Pope Pius XII
laid down the goal of the public economy in the following
terms: "to ensure the permanent satisfaction of man's needs
in goods and material services, directed in their turn to
raising the moral, cultural and religious level."

An economy of *needs* is one directed towards satisfying

---

10 Pope Pius XII, Allocution of March 7th, 1948.
11 Pope Pius XII, Allocution of March 25th, 1949, to the members of the International
Labor Office.

the "fundamental" needs of man; like food, clothing, housing, development of personality, education of children, healthy improvement of body and soul [12] and the real needs of man.

—thus, not an economy of *false needs*, artificially created by propaganda and advertising.

—not an economy of *lucre*, for the profit of the capitalist financier who overshadows the economic scene and himself determines which needs shall be satisfied. These needs are expressed in terms of money and are founded on financial means and buying capacity and are thus for the people who have, leaving unsatisfied many of the needs of those who have not the resources to procure the necessities of life.[13]

—not *an economy of luxury*. Pope Pius XII denounced at least twice (November 2nd, 1950, and March 8th, 1952), "the intolerable growth of luxury spending, unnecessary and unreasonable spending which contrasts bitterly with the misery of many."[14]

—not a purely *quantitative economy*, aiming above all at "an abundance of goods, their value calculated purely and simply on material standards." [15]

It is primarily a question of "relating production to consumption, wisely geared to the needs and dignity of man." [16]

---

12 Pope Pius XII, "There are needs which must be satisfied immediately; food, clothing, housing, education of children and the true restoration of body and soul." (Allocution to the Catholic Association of Italian workers, June 29th, 1948).

13 Pope Pius XII, "This is where the fundamental principles of economic liberalism also lead, *once the pursuit of lucre financial capitalism weighs down the economic* life and *when the implications of the national economy are considered only from the point of view of their market value.*" Allocution to the International Congress on Rural Life, July 2nd, 1951.

14 Pope Pius XII, Letter of July 5th, 1952, to M. Charles Flory.

15 Pope Pius XII, Radio Message, June 1st, 1941.

16 Pope Pius XII, Discourse of June 3rd, 1950, to the International Congress of Social Studies at the University of Fribourg.

One can see what the results of such principles would be. Production would no longer be solely for money and profit as it is in a capitalistic economy. It would no longer serve only the power, prestige and domination of the state as it does in the economy of the totalitarian state. Man would no longer be a mere robot or tool for production.

This is the perspective necessary to understand the severe judgment passed by Pius XII, following Pius XI, on liberal Capitalism: "Thus, as our glorious predecessor Pius XI showed in his Encyclical *Quadragesimo Anno,* it too often happens that *it is no longer human needs* which, according to their natural and objective importance, order the economic life and use of capital, but, on the contrary, it is capital and its ambitions for gain which determine which needs will be satisfied and to what extent. *In such circumstances it is not human work in the service of the common good which attracts and uses capital but, on the contrary, capital which disposes at its pleasure of both man and his work, like bowls in the hand of the player."* [17]

4) An economy which aims at improving, developing and perfecting human beings.

Pope Pius XII, speaking to the leaders of Italian industry at a Congress to study their mission in the economic reorganization of the South of Italy, (a region particularly poverty-stricken), showed them the goal to be achieved; the end that individuals aim at, and to which the state as such is ordained, is the true improvement of a people and, in consequence,

---

[17] Pope Pius XII, Allocution to Italian farmers, November 15, 1956.

the achievement of their lawful economic, social and cultural autonomy.[18] And thus the economy would be one of human progress, of "material prosperity for the whole population," [19] "a prosperity which in itself also constitutes a solid basis for cultural and religious life."

The economy would be for the worker's betterment because "the working class, in that which concerns it, is called to-day to take on responsibilities it never knew in the past." [20]

Such a human economy would aim at raising the standards of living and the purchasing power of the workers would give the working class the chance to take its place, "its responsible part in the running of the national economy." [21] "with equal rights with regard to the other members" [22] and "access to the full exercise of its responsibilities." [23] There is a duty to raise this class of men, who are exposed to economic hazards, to the level of other classes in society with defined rights.[24]

Pius XII deplored the fact that workers should be as strangers in the economic life of the nation. They have the feeling that they are on the fringe of society. The pope defended the principle that the working class should have a say in the management of economy. He based this view on the community of interest and responsibility between all those who take part in production. He wanted the workers to

18 Pope Pius XII, Allocution of June 6th, 1955.
19 Pope Pius XII, Discourse to Italian workers, March 11th, 1945.
20 Pope Pius XII, Letter to Canon Cardjin, March 21st, 1949.
21 Pope Pius XII, Discourse to Italian workers, March 11th, 1945.
22 Pope Pius XII, Allocution to the 1st Italian Congress on Women workers, August 15th, 1945.
23 Pope Pius XII, Discourse to the Italian Labor Organization, November, 1954.
24 Pope Pius XII, Radio Message to Austrian Catholics, September 14th, 1952.

have a just and responsible part in the setting up and development of social economy.

In *Mater et Magistra*, John XXIII expresses the desire for closer participation of workers in their enterprises:

"Furthermore, as did our predecessors, we regard as justifiable the desire of employees to be partners in enterprises with which they are associated and wherein they work. We do not think it possible, however, to decide with certain and explicit norms the manner and degree of such partnership, since this must be determined according to the state of the individual productive enterprise. . . . Nevertheless, we do not doubt that employees should have an active part in the affairs of the enterprise wherein they work, whether these be private or public. But it is of the utmost importance that productive enterprises assume the character of a true human fellowship whose spirit suffuses the dealings, activities, and standing of all its members. This requires that mutual relations between employers and directors on the one hand and the employees of the enterprise on the other, be marked by mutual respect, esteem, and good will. It also demands that all collaborate sincerely and harmoniously in their joint undertaking, and that they perform their work not merely with the objective of deriving an income, but also of carrying out the role assigned them and of performing a service that results in benefit to others. This means that the workers may have a say in, and may make a contribution toward, the efficient running and development of the enterprise." [25]

---

25 M.M., 91-92.

A fundamental point of the Church's social doctrine is the raising of man through the full development of all his faculties and attributes, spiritual and physical. This is the sacred and obligatory end of every social economy. It is the first of the essential right of the human person which Pius XII listed. But Marx accused the Church of not wanting any improvement in the lives of the workers and of only preaching resignation and passive acceptance of their fate. What a horrible calumny, replied Pope Pius XII, who himself frequently demonstrated all that the Church had done and called for in the establishment of a more just social economy where the workers could, at last, live like human beings. It also often happens that the Church's teaching on the duty of giving men the *"greatest possible spiritual and material well-being* in this life"[26] is ignored.

The Church is accused of being uninterested in men's earthly welfare in her concern for their heavenly good. The pope's reply: Man was put into a social life so that, by fully cultivating his faculties to the glory of his Creator and faithfully fulfilling the duties of his profession or vocation, "he may ensure both his temporal and eternal happiness."[27] Here is how Pius XII describes the social order at its best: "that all should be *subjects,* and lawfully participate in the formation of the social order and that all, following their art and their profession, can live peacefully and happily with sufficient means of existence. . ."[28]

5) A human economy is one which makes its benefits *available to all men.*

---

26 Pope Pius XI, Encyclical, Divini Illius Magistri.
27 Pope Pius XI Encyclical, Quadragesimo Anno.
28 Pope Pius XII, Allocution, September 12th, 1948.

The end of the social economy is "to make available to all men, in a consistent fashion, the material conditions necessary for the development of their cultural and spiritual lives." [29]

Thus it cannot be an economy reserved for the privileged, nor for a financial oligarchy, nor for an economic dictatorship, as Pius XI pointed out in the third part of Quadragesimo Anno. Neither can it be an autarchical society, thinking only of its own people. It must be open to all in the spirit of international co-operation and friendliness for which Pius XII ceaselessly called.[30]

6) A human economy should *fit man* and *be made to human scale*.

Is not this the preoccupation which alerted the popes to the danger to the human person presented by impersonal and gigantic collective enterprises, either capitalist or socialist, in which man disappears as a person and becomes nothing more than a cog in the huge machine? Of course the pope recognized the marvellous results in these of the inventive and constructive power of the human mind. But he denounced the perils that may follow for man himself, the family and society.

Is it not the same anxiety which moved Pius XII to express his preference for the small or medium-sized enterprises where personal responsibility is directly involved and for an economy in which factories are more accessible to man, to his home, and less centralized?

Some will say; "a beautiful dream, but impracticable,

---

29 Pope Pius XII, Allocution March 7th, 1948, to the Congress on International Exchange.
30 Pope Pius XII, particularly messages of December 24th, 1941 and December 24th, 1952.

the current is too strong and it carries all before it. Technical and productive processes require the centralization of industry. The movement of history is towards centralization in industry, finance and commerce."

It can be replied, first of all, that the pope was conversant with the economic facts and knew well how to judge the situation *as it is*. His mission is to recall to men, in the name of the moral law, what *it ought to be*—at least the ideal—to which the requirements of humanity should be brought as close as possible.

But there is more to it than that. Who would dare to pretend that the progress of true civilization, the material necessities of the people which require a nation to use its natural resources to the best advantage, a deeper realization of the real wants of man, would not influence governments, economists, politicians and industrialists to look for other and more human solutions. Surely this is the inspiration which has already given rise to so many plans for the development of under-exploited areas, town-planning, investment, decentralization, the location of industry and other projects of economic expansion? What may tomorrow bring if man succeeds in fully mastering atomic energy and automation? [31]

So much so that, contrary to the theories which held good up to the War of 1940, an eminent French philosopher and social economist declared that "If France wants to develop the dynamism for balanced economic expansion she must turn her back on the industrial, financial and commer-

---

31 There has been a real, if small, movement towards decentralisation in France. There have been efforts to help industry in remote areas and to distribute factories and industries more rationally throughout the country—all of which become possible with modern economic and industrial techniques. The regions are being devoloped to the profit of the country as a whole.

cial expansion of the last century" (M. Charles Flory, at the opening of the Social Study Week in Marseilles, July, 1956).

The relevance of a human economy

If we wish to understand the relevance of the Church's social teaching it is sufficient to examine the present trends of economic science. Forty years ago students of political economy learned that it was the science of wealth, values and prices. A purely scientific concept prevailed, founded on a mechanical physical analysis of economic phenomena.

Today the efforts of eminent economists to understand the real needs of man and to integrate him into the study of economic mechanisms so that he becomes the center of economic science, which, in turn, becomes the science of human activity, is both heartening and promising. It is enough to read the works of Henri Guitton,[32] Francois Perroux,[33] Andre Piettre [34] and Jean Marchal,[35] to mention only professors in the State Universities. But, in justice, we must also mention the considerable influence exercised by the studies of Fr. Lebret and "Economie et humanisme," of "Action Populaire" with Fathers Desbuquois, Villain and Bigo, with the eminent professors of the Catholic Universities who all try to develop the papal directives towards a more human economy.

---

32 Henri Guitton, Professor in the Faculty of Law, Paris.
33 Francois Perroux, Professor in the Faculty of Law, Paris.
34 Andre Piettre, Professor in the Faculty of Law, Paris.
35 Jean Marchal, Professor in the Faculty of Law, Paris.
    Some English equivalents of the authors mentioned here would be Colin Clark, "Welfare and Taxation," (Catholic Social Guild, 1954); Alfred Marshall, "Principles of Economics" (Prentice Hall); Michael Fogarty, "Economic Control" (Routledge & Keegan Paul).

Second Characteristic

AN ECONOMY FOR THE COMMON GOOD

"Accordingly, advances in social organization can and should be so brought about that maximum advantages accrue to citizens while at the same time disadvantages are averted or at least minimized. That these desired objectives be more readily obtained, it is necessary that public authorities have a correct understanding of the common good. This embraces the sum total of those conditions of social living, whereby men are enabled more fully and more readily to achieve their own perfection. —Mater et Magistra, 64-65.

The doctrine of the common good is one of the fundamental bases of the social teaching of the Church. Originally it belonged solely to the Church's social teaching. Soon the value of its ideas captivated minds far removed from Catholicism. Statesmen took it as their inspiration and it was incorporated into currents of opinion and social ideas. Yet it is important not to allow the frequent misuse of the term, emptied of its moral connotations, to distort its true meaning.

Four points arise:

1) What is the common good?
2) What are its essential components?
3) Greatness of the common good.
4) Service of the common good and the State.

I. WHAT IS THE COMMON GOOD?

Pope Pius XII defined it as: to realize, in a lasting fashion and to *"preserve, develop and perfect the human person by facilitating the due fulfilment and realization of the religious and cultural laws and values which the Creator has assigned to every man and to the human race."* [1]

The word "good" has a special meaning in the social teaching of the Church. It is usually used in preference to the term "general *interest.*" This latter indeed conjures up for many the idea of purely material and quantitative advantages without taking quality into account. It has a connotation of egotistical gain and personal profit without reference to whether they are honest or lawful. An example will illustrate this. How many people, purporting to invoke the general interest of the nation, do not hesitate to defend the entrepeneurs of the narcotics business and the shameful profiteers of the white slave traffic and public brothels, etc. Those who understand the general interest only in financial terms hold that it benefits the nation to let such enterprises flourish because they can yield taxes and special levies. In reality, such undertakings work only towards the nation's destruction.

Of course the common good is the lasting realization of exterior conditions and it includes material things. But the name "good" has a moral significance and implies moral values. The "good" is that which perfects a human person ... that which perfects, achieves, and completes him as a

---

1 Pope Pius XII, Radio Message, December 24th, 1942.

rational and free human being ... that which provides the satisfaction not only of his material and physical needs but also of his noble aspirations as a man the satisfaction of his intellectual, artistic, cultural and spiritual needs and thus provides peace, security, confidence and happiness.

Leo XIII set out the doctrine in these terms: "without any doubt the common good, whose acquisition should have the effect of *perfecting* men, is principally a moral good." [2]

The common good is defined in relation to man; it is the human good of a human community, whether family, professional, national or international. We will consider here the common good of the national community.

The common good is this human good, as we have defined it, applied to a human community. It is a general good, a good which is ensured by *general* outside conditions for the *general mass* of the people. It is a good which members of the national community should seek and bring about together, because it answers the essential need of the human beings. All men are called to enjoy its benefits together because they are conferred on each man as a member of the social body. The common good requires the members of the national community to go beyond the particular or collective interests of political parties or professional or specialized groups so that they can establish conditions favorable to the life of the nation and to its prosperity, its greatness, its place in the community of nations and its mission in the service of mankind.

---

2 Pope Leo XIII, Encyclical, Rerum Norarum.

II. WHAT ARE THE ESSENTIAL COMPONENTS OF
THE COMMON GOOD?

A thorough study of papal teaching allows us to distinguish three essential components of the common good:

1) public order,

2) prosperity,

3) intellectual, spiritual and moral values.

1) *A public and external order.*

Pope Pius XII, defining the end to which the social economy tends, (which is none other than the common good) declared that this end "is to make available in a stable manner, to all members of society, the necessary material conditions to develop their cultural and spiritual life."[3] The pope added; "Here, it is not possible to get any results without an *external order*, without the social norms which aim at obtaining this end and keeping it."[4]

The common good therefore presupposes a public, external order which would ensure protection of life and property, respect for freedoms and rights, defense of the country by land, sea and air, and the exercise of justice by honest judges.

The pope underlined the need for stability and permanence in the conditions of this public state. Nothing is more dangerous to the common good than upheavals, revolutions and crises in the government which has the responsibility for this public order.

The pope also taught the necessity of having a *judicial*

---

3 Discourse to members of the Congress on International Exchange, March, 7th, 1948.
4 Ibid.

status to give this social life an external backing and protection and to guide the particular energies of all citizens in their co-operation for the common good. This public order would also afford a guarantee of security for all men.[5]

2) *Material prosperity for the whole population.*

"The national economy, by its regular and peaceful development opens the way *to material prosperity for the whole population.*" [6] Pope John XXIII enumerates the principal components of common good: "Considering the common good on the national level, the following points are relevant and should not be overlooked: to provide employment for as many workers as possible; to take care lest privileged groups arise even among the workers themselves; to maintain a balance between wages and prices; to make accessible the goods and services for a better life to as many persons as possible; either to eliminate or to keep within bounds the inequalities that exist between different sectors of the economy—that is, between agriculture, industry and services; to balance properly any increases in output with advances in services provided to citizens, especially by public authority; to adjust, as far as possible, the means of production to the progress of science and technology; finally, to ensure that the advantages of a more humane way of

---

5 "In order that social life should attain the end wished for it by God it must have a judicial status as a help, refuge and protection, whose role it is to help and not dominate this social life and to develop and strengthen the vitality of society in the multiplicity of its objectives, directing individual energies in peaceful competition and defending them by all lawful and appropriate means against whatever would inhibit their full development." Radio Message, June 1st, 1941.
6 Pope Pius XII, Discourse to Italian workers, March 11th, 1945.

existence not merely subserve the present generation but have regard for future generations as well." [7]

Earlier, Pope Leo XIII laid down the role of governments and the state in the encyclical *Rerum Novarum*: "The foremost duty of the rulers of the state should be to make sure that the laws and institutions, the general character and administration of the commonwealth, shall be such as of themselves to realize *public well-being and private prosperity.*"

What does this prosperity require? First of all the material elements which the citizens can use in common or in which they share a sufficiency of produce, goods and commodities ... easy communciation by land, sea and air ... a prudent organization of production to answer real needs, "the most balanced developments of all the means of production over the whole territory inhabited by the same people," [8] the prosperity of industry, agriculture, commerce and trades ... an equitable distribution of the national revenue between the different social groups, "a just and proper sharing by everyone in the wealth of the country...," [9] "an improvement in the standards of living of the different classes in the nation and most particularly the popular masses, with an increase in their purchasing power for the most depressed sections ... a clear, just and moderate fiscal policy ... financial equilibrium and a stable and strong currency which enjoys public confidence."

But the prosperity of a people lies not so much in these elements of the material, economic and social order as in

---

7 M.M., 79.
8 Pope Pius XII, Discourse to the International Congress on International Exchange, March 7th, 1948.
9 Pope Pius XII, Discourse to Italian workers, June 13th, 1943.

fruitful, united families playing their part with others in life . . . in its eager youth at work . . . in an atmosphere of social peace and security, of loyal collaboration between the different professions for the common good, [10] in a climate favorable to the flowering of intellectual, spiritual and moral values.

3) *Higher values of the intellectual, spiritual, moral and religious order.*

The common good of a nation calls on the combined forces of savants, inventors, thinkers, intellectuals, and scientists.

In the intellectual and moral order, the common good of society demands general education, the development of intellectual, humanistic or technical training, culture and different forms of art. The common good requires that the souls, consciences, will and energies of young people should be developed to awaken in them a strong, balanced and disciplined personality. Youth must be trained to submit its whims and passions to a higher law, to practise virtue and give itself to a high and noble ideal. This whole work of integral education presupposes the love of the good, of the true and the beautiful and the struggle against egoism, laziness and cowardice.

The popes recalled the primordial place and good influence of the moral virtues among the essential elements of the common good: loyalty, courage, honor, patriotism, professional ethics and the love of work. Pope Pius XII

---

10 Pope Pius XI, Encyclical, Divini Illius Magistri.

insisted on a full, personal "responsibility in the temporal order as well as in the eternal." [11]

Speaking of social reforms "such as are urgently required by the necessities and desires of our times," the pope declared that; "some require a spirit of renunciation and sacrifice, others a sense of responsibility and endurance and all call for hard and arduous work." [12]

Finally, the common good, as envisaged by the social teaching of the Church, puts respect for religion in the first place because of what it is, the homage rendered to God. It is the supreme good also by virtue of its influence on men's minds, their families and social contacts and the way in which it educates them in the meaning of the common good. Leo XIII wrote, "to procure the common good is to make religion esteemed above all else and to extend its influence, so natural and marvellously salutary, to political, domestic and economic interests." [13]

III.   THE GREATNESS AND IMPORTANCE OF THE COMMON GOOD.

All the popes have taught the importance, the necessity and the greatness of the common good. Leo XIII said of the common good "This good, is, after God, the first and last law in society." [14]

Pius XI showed how the common good was called for by the social nature of man and the end of society: "The true common good is determined and recognized, in the last

---

11 Radio Message, December 24th, 1942.
12 Allocution to the Sacred College, June 2nd, 1948.
13 Leo XIII, Encyclical, Permoti Nos.
14 Leo XIII, "In the midst of cares," February 16th, 1892.

analysis, by *the nature of man* which harmoniously balances personal rights *and social* duties and by *the end of society,* also determined by this same human nature .... To deviate from this order is to overthrow the pillars on which society rests and thus to jeopardize the tranquility, security and very existence of society." [15]

Pope Pius XII, who frequently defined the common good, taught that one of its essential principles was, "the *overriding requirement* of society to place the common good beyond personal advantage, the service of each for all." [16]

The greatness of the common good lies in the fact that it is in accordance with *God's plan* which united all men in a common nature and put them to live in society. Men were destined to make use of the conditions of their life in common to direct them towards the good and to pursue their destiny by helping each other.

The common good of society is great also because the good which conditions the existence, vitality, well-being and happiness of a people is greater than individual or particular goods, limited to their own sphere of families, professions or groups. It alone can realize the unity and greatness of a nation. It has a universal scope and effectiveness and applies not only within every section of society but also to the relations of the sections with each other.

Another aspect of the greatness of the common good is that its role is to "safeguard the intangible domain of the rights of the human person and to help him fulfil his duties." [17] It is great because it is addressed to man as a whole, to invite

---

15 Pius XI, Encyclical on Nazism, "Mit Brennender Sorge."
16 Pius XII, Allocution of July 16th, to the U.S. delegates to the International Labor Office. Also M.M., 78.
17 Pius XII, Message, June 1st, 1941.

him to reach out to realize his destiny, to fulfil himself in helping others to become better, more free and human, to discipline his selfishness, to rise above his petty personal interests, to take his responsibilities in the social body and to practise all the virtues included in the giving of self to this higher ideal. Social justice animates all the virtues which make up the greatness of man and puts them at the service of the common good.[18]

The greatness of the common good lies in the fact that it is addressed *to all men,* to all families and all societies which are encouraged to emulate each other and to *co-ordinate all their efforts.* It has in itself a power to work wonderful changes in the life of a nation and to ensure its social rehabilitation.

The greatness of the common good is that, far from shutting a nation in on itself, it calls it to co-operate for the international common good and the good of all mankind.

Finally, since the supreme common good is God Himself, the search for the common good, prepares men to turn towards the Father of all who should Himself, after having been their most consistent good here on earth, be a "magnificent recompense" hereafter.

IV.   THE SERVICE OF THE COMMON GOOD.

Because of its greatness and importance the common good should be sought, loved and served by all citizens. It is the object of this higher charity, of which Pius XI said;

---

18 Pope Pius XI, "The Pubic institutions of the nations must be such as to make the whole of human society *conform to the needs of the common good, that is, to the standard of social justice."* (Quadragesimo Anno).

"such is the domain of the body politic which considers the interests of socitey as a whole and which on this account is the field of the most vast charity, of political charity, of which it can be said that no charity is greater except that of religion." [19]

The State. However, the service of the common good is primarily the proper mission of the state and of governments.

Leo XIII wrote: "considered in its nature, the civil power is set up to attend to the common good which is the supreme end that gives human society its origin." [20] And again: "The civil authority should not, under any pretext, serve to the advantage of one or a few, because it was *constituted for the common good.*" [21]

Pope Pius XII declared that this was the soul of ovory state. "The intimate and profound sense of the common good is the soul of every state." [22] All the activities of the state are pre-ordained to this end. "All economic and political activity of the state is ordered towards the lasting realization of the common good." [23] Better still: "This common good is *the end* and *the principle* of the state and of its organs." [24]

How can the state fulfil this mission towards the common good? By its laws and institutions and the services which stem from its government and administration. "The mission of the state is to control, help and regulate the private and

19 Pius XI, Discourse to the Italian University Catholic Federation, December 18th, 1927.
20 Leo XIII, "In the midst of cares," February 16th, 1892.
21 Leo XIII, Immortale Dei, 1885.
22 Pope Pius XII, Radio Message to the Swiss people, September 15th, 1946.
23 Pope Pius XII, Radio Message, December 24th, 1942.
24 Pope Pius XII, Discourse to the Roman aristocracy, January 8th, 1947. Also Mater et Magistra 20, 21.

individual activities of national life to make them converge harmoniously for the common good." [25]

The state should first of all "have equal care for all classes of its citizens strictly observing the laws of distributive justice" [26] and protecting the rights of one and all.

It ought nevertheless to realize that "the weak and poor have a claim to special consideration. The richer class have many ways of shielding themselves, and stand less in need of help from the State; whereas the mass of the poor have no resources of their own to fall back upon, and must chiefly depend upon the assistance of the State. And it is for this reason that wage-earners, since they mostly belong to that class, should be specially cared for and protected by the government." [27] Leo XIII also taught the important position of the workers. "Justice, therefore, demands that the interests of the working-classes should be carefully watched over by the administration. . . . It follows that whatever shall appear to prove conducive to the well-being of those who work should obtain favorable consideration. There is no fear that solicitude of this kind will be harmful to any interest: on the contrary, it will be to the advantage of all; for it cannot but be good for the commonwealth to shield from misery those on whom it so largely depends for the things that it needs." [28] Thus it is the desire for the common good which imposes a particular duty on the State to protect the mass of workers by its laws.

---

25 Pope Pius XII, Encyclical, Summi Pontificatus.
26 Leo XIII, Rerum Novarum.
27 Pius XI, Quadragesimo Anno.
28 Leo XIII, Rerum Novarum.

In conclusion: Three remarks are useful here.

1. It is superfluous to underline the *relevance* and the urgent necessity of this chapter of the Church's social teaching. The main reason for the decadence of society is that to-day the common good is ignored, disowned, ridiculed and betrayed. There is a race for selfish pleasure and a coalition of private and corporate interests against the common good. "Every man for himself." "Get to the top by any means—but get there." Except for a small elite, the great majority of men have lost the sense of service for the common good.

As we indicated at the beginning of this chapter there has been a lamentable confusion between two concepts. The spiritual concept of the common good has been too long eclipsed by the materialistic concept of the general interest. To talk of the general interest is to interpolate and add particular interests; meanness, selfishness, hedonism and self-interest all enter in. In making known the idea of the common good the popes' teaching has unmasked the false meaning.

2. Are we sufficiently aware of the considerable influence wielded by the popes' interventions against liberalism and in favor of social legislation by the state, which brought just reforms into the workers' lives?

Two dates should be noted. The Encyclical was in 1891 —but the first French labor law to protect women and children at work dates from 1892 and was initiated by a Catholic, de Mun.

In *Quadragesimo Anno*, Pius XI described the extraordinary impression made by Rerum Novarum on statesmen, parliamentarians and on the masses themselves.[29]

---

29 "Nor was the Apostolic voice vain. It was listened to with admiration . . . . . not

3. There is not the same difficulty in getting public opinion to accept the state's intervention today. On the contrary, the danger lies in the opposite direction—excessive centralization and a statism which jeopardises the rights of the human person. That is why Pius XII ranked the state's protection of these rights to be of the first importance: "To safeguard the intangible domain of the human person and to help him to fulfil his duties should be the primary role of all public power. Surely this is the true meaning of the common good that the state is called upon to promote." [30]

---

only by loyal children of the Church but ... by Christian working-men. . . . . .and by all those devoted men whose concern it had long been to better the conditions of labor." Pius XI, Quadragesimo Anno.

30 Pope Pius XII, Radio Message, June 1st, 1941; also Mater et Magistra, 66.

Third Characteristic

AN ORGANIC ECONOMY

I. It is an *organic* economy, first in the sense that it should help to give society the *unity of an organism*. "The economy of a people is an organic whole; an organic whole in which all the productive possibilities of national territory should be developed in a wise and balanced fashion." (Pius XII, 15-11-1946)

The popes sought to inspire men to apply to the social body St. Paul's image of the unity of the physical body. As in the physical body the members work in the unity of the whole through the diversity of their functions. Thus the organic concept of the economy should seek the necessary unity of the social organism beyond diversities of work, professions and classes so that a single body is formed.[1]

Nevertheless, as Pius XII specified, if the comparison with the physical body is useful as a starting point, it should be quickly outstripped when it is applied to the social community, because of the dignity of every human being. In the physical organism, the organs are integrated parts of the whole and have no meaning or end in themselves. The unity of the whole exists in itself even if an organ is lacking.

---

1 Pope Pius XII, January 31st, 1952 and Allocution of March 7th, 1948, to Congress on International Exchange.

In the community of men, on the contrary, each human person has his own dignity and his personal destiny. He is not merely an organ, an instrument, or a cog in the wheel. The members of the community form a *unity of purpose and action* in the sense that they are, by the wise use of their freedom and consciousness of their solidarity, co-operators and instruments for the achievement of the common good.[2]

By this organic concept of the social economy, the Church's social teaching reacts, on the one hand, against the abuses of an over-individualistic view of the liberal economy and, on the other, against an over-organized concept of society which can trample on the human person and man's conscience.[3]

In considering the ideal of the unity of the moral community, the popes came up against and analyzed the brutal fact of class warfare. They have all described the deplorable results of this conflict, which makes impossible the establishment of this unity of the body which is necessary for life itself.

This is why the Church teaches that there is a *community of interests higher* than the diversity of functions and the different interests which naturally follow. There is a solidarity between all those, employers and workers, masters and servants, directors and staff, who work together in the same line of business. The Church sees between them "a higher unity ... to know their interdependence and common interest in their duty to work together consistently for

---

2 Pius XII, Allocution to the Congress on the histo-pathology of the nervous system, September 14th, 1952.

3 Pius XII, Radio Message, December 24th, 1952.

the common good and the needs of the whole community." And Pius XII expressed the Church's will on this point: "This solidarity should extend to all branches of production and become the basis of *a better economic order.*" [4] The Pope saw "the foundation of the future social order" [5] in this higher unity between all those who contribute to production.

Here we come across a widespread objection. "Class warfare exists. Indeed it is capitalism which provoked it. It is an historical fact. The only way for the working-class to put an end to the injustice with which it is victimized is to go right into the war against the capitalists. Appeals for understanding between the classes are sentimental illusions which benefit only those in possession."

Reply: 1. It is true that class warfare exists beween employers and workers and that it for too long reacted in favor of the wealthy.

It is no less true that the working-class has had to fight for its freedoms and betterment by strikes which showed the strength of organized force.

Finally, it is certain that there will always be tensions between different classes and groups of human beings. Some of these are even beneficial. The problem is to reconcile them in terms of justice and the common good.

But war between nations is also a fact of all ages and nevertheless the Church has not resigned herself to it but has always desired and preached peace in justice and right. The system of wars is being gradually replaced by that of peaceful relations between nations and who will deny that

---

4 Pope Pius XII, Allocution to Italian workers, March 11th, 1945
5 Pope Pius XII, Allocution of January 25th, 1946

this would represent an enormous step forward in human progress? Every substitution of right for force marks a victory for mankind. If this be the case, why cannot this progress in international relations be extended to relations between the classes? "Class warfare should be overcome by the inauguration of an organic order uniting owners and workers." [6]

2. It would be wrong and confusing to suppose that the Church by her teaching calls for an end to the struggle for justice. The two things are quite different. Christians have no right to resign themselves to injustice. Pope Pius XII recalled [7] that the Church "always fought loyally to *defend the human rights of the workers.* Fought loyally—because the Church believed herself *obliged before God and by the law of Christ* to do so. Fought loyally—not to stir up class hatred but to guarantee the working-class a position as sure and lasting as that already enjoyed by other classes and ranks."

3. We must go further. Class warfare should be ended not just because the forces of each side are so evenly balanced that they are stabilized in a sort of cold war, but because all classes should *together fight for social justice*—which is the greatest good. *Each one should co-operate according to his means to bring it about* just as all nations should achieve peace together and co-operate in its establishment.

It has not been sufficiently noted that this union of the classes, constantly advocated and called for by the popes, should come about *in view of an objective which is too great*

6 Pope Pius XII, Radio Message to Austrian Catholics, September 14th, 1952
7 Pope Pius XII, Allocution to the first Italian congress of women workers August 15th, 1945

for any one of them to accomplish singly. This objective is that of the common good and needs of the whole community.[8] This requires the help of employers and capitalists as well as of the workers. The surest way to block it and intensify the struggle is to consistently resist all reasonable demands for change. Furthermore, this common good is concerned not only with relations between two classes but also with the whole economic, social and political structure.

II. It is also *organic* economy in the sense that it is based on *vocational organization* in all branches of production. The importance of intermediary bodies between the state and the individual is a key idea in the Church's social teaching. These bodies are nearer to the true needs of man and are more easily able to make the best use of his personal initiative and responsibility. They keep the state from becoming top-heavy.

Leo XIII, in *Rerum Novarum*, affirmed the natural right of association and declared that the state should respect and protect the right of associations to govern themselves as long as they were not contrary to the common good. It was at the time a daring act for the pope because public authorities had been for a long time refusing this right to workers' groups.[9]

Nevertheless Leo XIII did not yet formalize a type of vocational organization. He aimed at composite societies, either of workers only or of both workers and employers.

Pius XI, in *Quadragesimo Anno*, indicated a definite

---

8 Pope Pius XII, Allocution, January 25th, 1946
9 In France, corporations were abolished in 1791. Workers only gained the right to strike in 1864 and had to wait until 1884 for the right to form trade unions.

formula "'*corporative*' vocational organization." It underlined the *evil* of the bitter war between the classes. The
remedy as he saw it lay in basing the social life on vocational
lines and not on distinctions of class. The *instrument* would
be the organization of vocational bodies which would be
like the organs of society (if not *essential* and constitutional
like the family or the civil society, at least *natural* and in
conformity with the needs of human nature). The *end* of
this vocational organization would be the search for the
common good of the group and its direction to the common
good of society.

Pope Pius XII took up the program of vocational
organization and defined it. He underlined its importance
in an Allocution of 1952 when he protested against those
who applied certain extracts of his predecessor's Encyclical
to themselves while they passed over in silence "the principal
part of the Encyclical, *Quadragesimo Anno,* which contains
this program i.e. the idea of the corporative vocational order
of the whole economy." [10]

What is important, said the pope, is "to work in good
faith and fervently for the realization of the thing itself
and its many practical applications."

---

10 Allocution to members of the Christian Union of leaders of Italian Industry,
January 31st, 1952. It is important to note that this word "corporative" has certain
Fascist connotations for some people in France and Italy.

It is important therefore to remember that in Quadragesimo Anno, Pius XI,
denounced the "excessively bureaucratic and political character" of Mussolini's corporative organization and the fact that, notwithstanding its general advantages,
"it ends in serving particular political aims rather than ... a better social order"
Pius XII later made it quite clear that there was no intention of attempting to return
to the Middle Ages—which is another connotation of the word for some. Certainly
the popes never intended the word "corporative" to start controversies which might
obscure the nature of the reforms which are necessary; and indeed they more frequently use the word "vocational."

Pius XII saw, in this reform, "a new grouping of the productive forces of the people."[11]

In the pope's teaching on this point it is useful to distinguish three closely linked problems: the trade union, the vocational organization and the legal status of professional bodies.

1. THE TRADE UNIONS.

The Pope spoke frequently about them. He defined the aim, their raison d'etre and their legality.

Their primary aim is to "defend the worker's interests in labor agreements."[12]

Their raison d'etre is that "they arose as a spontaneous and necessary result of capitalism as an economic system." Their legality has been affirmed on numerous occasions by the Church. Speaking to Italian workers, Pius XII said: "In the trade union as such you see a solid support for the economic society of our time which has been more than once recognized in the social teaching of the Church."[13]

The trade unions recognized as necessary by the Church are those which, while they defend the workers' rights and interests, try to overcome class-warfare by working towards a constructive program which takes into account the general state of economy. Under this heading they can be the natural basic organs of vocational organization;

---

11 Allocution to members of Congress of the Christian Association of Italian Workers, March 11th, 1945.
12 Allocution to the Workers' Christian Movement of Belgium, September 11th, 1949
13 Again Discourse to Italian Workers, June 29th, 1948

different unions of owners, managers, technicians, workers and employees.[14]

2. THE VOCATIONAL ORGANIZATION.

Its *end* is to set up normal, regular and organic *links* between members of the same business so that they can all work together for the good of the vocational group and that of the whole community, no matter how different their work or place within the group may be.

Pius XII distinguished two planes on which members should come together: that of the profession or business and that of the national community.

The *common good of the profession or business* in which all the members are interested (workers, managers, directors, etc.) is that the profession or business should be stable and prosperous, that it should have good markets and outlets, that it should enable each of its members to lead a full human life and that their professional or business relations should be based on justice and loyal co-operation.

But many vocational groups consider only their own interest and advantage. This is one of the most striking signs of the present friction within the state. "Whether it is a question of employers' or workers' unions, of economic trusts or of professional or social groups (some of them even in the service of the state), these organizations have acquired a power which enables them to exert pressures on the government and the national life." [15]

---

14 Mater et Magistra 23, 97
15 Pope Pius XII, Letter of July 14th to the Social Week at Rennes.

That is why the pope underlined the duty of every profession to co-operate for the *common good of the national community*. The pope showed how workers and management in the same industry had a common interest in the national economy. "Management and workers are not irreconcilable antagonists. They are co-operators in a common task. They eat, so to speak, at the same table since they live, in the final analysis, from the net and gross profit of the national economy. Each gets his share as of right and on this account the one is not under an obligation to the other." [16] They all have an interest in seeing that the table is well laden. The national economy is a communal table from which everyone should take his portion whether in the form of profits, wages or salary. Profits and wages, which seem in conflict within a single industry, are both part of the national income.

From this viewpoint the workers are on the same plane as their employers and this provides equality of rights and duties.

Pius XII did not wish, any more than his predecessor, to pronounce on the *technical* problem of the structure of the vocational organization. The popes feel that this is not a question within the Church's competence. Men can organize whatever forms appear best to them. They are free to lay down the rules and statutes most appropriate to the national temperament and the needs of each country. There is no single, rigid formula other than that justice and the common good of the society should be guaranteed. It is well known how socially minded Catholics have devised different machinery for vocational organization—work committees,

---

16 Pope Pius XII, Allocution to members of the International Union of Catholic Employers, March 7th, 1949. Also Mater et Magistra, 98

mixed commissions and collective work conventions. Pius XII himself enumerated the different aspects of such organization in his Allocution of January 25, 1946.[17]

The Advantages of Vocational Organization

No matter what form vocational organization may take, the popes' teaching has illustrated the advantages it can confer.

First, thanks to vocational organization and its institutions, *social justice* becomes possible and more easily applied, for it keeps in check the type of competition which operates against the true interests of the workers.

Furthermore, vocational organization opens up to the workers the means of taking *their share of the responsibility* in the running of the national economy.

Finally, this great organization of vocational bodies, establishing as it does organic links between capital and labor, prepares the way for internal peace and harmony.

3. THE LEGAL STRUCTURE OF ECONOMIC AND SOCIAL LIFE ORGANIZED ON A PROFESSIONAL BASIS.

If we make the necessary adjustments we can apply here the rules which Pius XII assigned to the legal structure of society itself. "If social life, such as God wills it, is to attain its end it needs a legal structure for its *support, defense and protection.* The function of this structure is not to dominate but to serve." [18]

---

17 Allocution to owners and workers of the Italian electricity industry. Also Mater et Magistra, 22
18 Message of December 24th, 1942

This text can help us to understand better what is meant by the legal structure of a profession; which is not to say that this public legal structure will make the professional organization into an organism of the State. A law which recognizes a private organism does not thereby make it into a public organism.

For the chaotic system of free competition, dominated by profit, or the conflict between opposing interests, we must substitute a rule of right, institutions officially acknowledged by the state, and a charter determining the powers and necessary means to ensure the mission of the professional organization. It is essential that this legal structure should serve "as a support" to the profession to define its functions on the technical, social and economic plane,[19] to ensure its place in society and to provide it with the means of economic expansion. This structure must also serve as a "defense and protection" in giving the profession certain disciplinary powers with sanctions, either in interior disputes which always endanger the unity of the professional community, or in conflicts with other professions or, finally, in relations with public authorities so that the demands of the common good of both the profession and that of the national community may be met. Such a structure prevents the coalition of powerful interests, monopolies, trusts and cartels.

"The function of the structure is not to dominate but to serve" said Pius XII. The state should, by the official recognition of professional organizations, help those concerned to organize their own affairs and not take on the job

---

19 Some private French groups have already worked out the precise role of different jobs in a vocational organization.

itself. The state is not there to direct but to encourage and promote such initiatives by its social and economic policies.

Pius XII insisted on the distinction between *private and public* rights and drew some important consequences on the nature of enterprise that we will discuss later.

But first of all we must consider the principles of the pope's social teaching concerning relations between the state and private enterprise in view of the problem of production. It is a delicate question. It is easy to misrepresent the Holy Father's teaching if one or other point of the doctrine is omitted.

PLANNING

First Principle: *the Pope frequently affirmed and recalled the need to organize social life, and in particular, production. He strongly underlined the State's mission in this domain. He recognized the usefulness of planning under certain conditions.*

"A just control of production does not leave out of account the principle governing state intervention which was brought to light by our illustrious predecessor, Leo XIII, particularly under present conditions." [20]

In an Allocution to members of the Sacred College on the 2nd of June, 1948,[21] the pope reiterated the necessity for a *wise organization of production*. He particularly noted two things: first, the conditions of the national economy and then

---

20 Pope Pius XII, Letter to M. Charles Flory, July 19th, 1947. Also, Pope John XXIII, Mater et Magistra, 99
21 Pope Pius XII, Allocution to the Sacred College of Cardinals, June 2nd, 1948

the relations beween the national economies and the world market.

"All social reform is bound up with the question of wise organization of production. Relations between agriculture and industry in the different national economies and the relations of these with each other and the manner and degree to which each nation participates in the world market are all difficult problems which arise in a different form to-day from that of other ages. The rational solution of these problems depends on the productivity of each nation and, as a result, the well-being of the individual, for it is clear that where there is not sufficient production there cannot be sufficient to distribute."

On the 5th of July, 1952 the pope defined the state's function in the field of production.

"First of all the duty of increasing production and *distributing it wisely according to man's needs and dignity poses, as a question of prime importance, the control of the productive sector of the economy.* Thus, (without substituting oppressive power for the lawful autonomy of private enterprise) *the state undeniably has a co-ordinating role which is all the more necessary under present social conditions.*

"In particular, its help is needed to set up *that kind of political economy* which boosts the active *co-operation* of all and the growth of production which is the direct source of the national income."[22]

All these texts should not be forgotten or passed over when we examine the pope's position with regard to legiti-

22 Pope Pius XII, Letter to M. Charles Flory for the Social Study Week at Dijon.

mate planning. Speaking of "plans" Pius XII declared, "we freely recognize that, within just limits, they can be desirable and even necessary according to the circumstances."[23]

Second principle: *Even as he underlined the state's role in the organization of production the pope warned against the dangers of over-rigid planning and an inhuman technocracy.*

Some people are amazed by the pope's reservations with regard to these "plans" whose usefulness and necessity he nevertheless recognized. He gave his reasons clearly.

First *he feared the over-rigidity of plans* which did not take sufficient account of man, his rights and his personal and family needs.

"Human society is not a machine and it must not be made such, not even in the economic field.... Indeed modern society, which would plan and organize everything, being regarded as a machine, comes into conflict with something living and which therefore cannot be made subject to quantitative calculations. More precisely, it comes into conflict with those rights which by nature man exercises on his own and personal responsibility—that is, as the author of a new life of which he is always the custodian." [24]

The pope then cites the problems of the birth-rate and emigration which cause a profound conflict between the system and man's conscience.

He adds:

"These examples suffice to show how an organization inspired by cold calculation becomes the negation of life

---

23 Pope Pius XII, Allocution of August 5th, 1950 to the International Congress on Administration.
24 Pope Pius XII, Radio Message, Christmas, 1952

itself which it tries to confine within the narrow limits of fixed norms as though it were a mere statistical phenomenon."

The pope vigorously denounces:

"The rigid incomprehension of society inflexible in its measures, which it devises according to calculations like a machine, but crushes without pity."

That is why the pope demands that purely organizational experts should not have the last word.

"Who can fail to see in these conditions, the damage that would result if the final word in affairs of the state were left to purely organizational experts?" [25]

Of course their role is an important one. It can show results, but under certain conditions.

"Their work can contribute particularly to resolving the serious and widespread problems which affect the world, on conditions that they apply themselves to improving and strengthening true human values."

In the second place if the pope expressed some fears on the subject of plans it *was in so far as they reflected a stranglehold of the state.*

"Once more, what we reject *is the stranglehold of the state.*" [26]

"In some countries the state *is becoming a gigantic administrative machine. It extends its influence over almost every phase of life.* It would bring under its administration the whole gamut of political, economic, social and intellec-

25 Pope Pius XII, Allocution of August 5th, 1950
26 Pope Pius XII, Allocution of August 5th, 1950

tual life, from birth to death." The pope then denounced the evil which afflicts modern man, *"the despoiling of man's personality."* [27]

Finally, the pope feared "the danger that the state might be dominated by economic forces to the detriment of the common good" [28] and the use by a totalitarian state of these plans.

Experience has proved the fears of the pope to have been well-founded. Events in Soviet Russia have shown that the use of integral planning by a totalitarian state, hungry for economic power, can result in a cruel oppression of the individual. For Stalin the important thing was not the fulfilment of the essential needs of all men. Priority was given to those sectors of the economy which were best able to build up a collectivist economy. The experience of Russia and of Yugoslavia has established "the radical unsuitability (explicitly recognized in Yugoslavia since 1952) of a policy of state centralized and integrated planning as a means of answering the economic needs of the people. The myth of integral planning having been shaken, the search for more flexible formulae was greatly helped" [29]... *Planning had been the work of a team of technocrats completely devoted to the political party in power*. The two points of view, that of men's needs and that of the building of a powerful collectivist economy, are as radically and intrinsically different as are men's needs and the pursuit of the maximum profit.

Integral planning is therefore no solution for it is

---

27 Pope Pius XII, Radio Message, Christmas, 1952
28 Pope Pius XII, Letter of July 19th, 1947, to M. Charles Flory for the Social Study Week in Paris.
29 M. Gilbert Blardone at the Social Study Week in Marseilles, 1956

incompatible with the common good. Other formulae which are more flexible and avoid the very dangers denounced by the pope can and should be studied.

NATIONALIZATION

The same reasons lay behind the pope's caution with regard to certain public and judicial forms of organization of the national economy, particularly *state ownership and the nationalization of industry*.

Not that he rejected them a priori. Like Pius XI he held that the Church allows them within certain just limitations and "it is rightly contended that *certain forms of property must be reserved to the state, since they carry with them a power too great to be left to private individuals without injury to the community at large*." [30]

But the pope did not accept state ownership as the normal rule of the public organization of the economy. This would be "a reversal of the right order of things; the mission of the public right is, in effect, to serve private right and not to absorb it."

In another discourse [31] Pius XII stated the cases in which nationalization is permissible. "Cases in which it is truly called for by the common good as the only really effective way to remedy an abuse or to avoid wasting the productive resources of the country and to ensure the organic control of these same resources to direct them to the best economic advantages of the nation." Thus, it is permissible, on the one hand, to remedy the abuse of mis-

---

30 Encyclical, Quadragesimo Anno
31 Pope Pius XII, Allocution to Italian Workers, March 11th, 1945

management which would waste resources indispensable to the nation. On the other hand it is permissible to ensure that the general interest should predominate in industries vital to the economic life of the nation.

Here again we find that marvellous balance which characterizes all the Church's social teaching. She gives the state a place of primary importance and considers it "as a moral organization, founded on the moral order of the world." [32] "as one of the constituent elements of the natural law." [33] But on the other hand she demands that this natural law should always inspire the state's laws and that the state should therefore always respect the rights and free initiative of individuals, families and groups.

Structural Reforms of Enterprise

Finally, the principle of the distinction between private and public right is again involved by Pius XII in the problem of structural reform of enterprise.

The pope demanded that these reforms should be studied with care and due regard for justice and equity. In the midst of the War he proclaimed his duty to be "to warn nations and their leaders that after these disasters they will *have to build an economic and social order more in accord with divine law and human dignity*, uniting the postulates of true justice and Christian principles in close unity and guaranteeing salvation, well-being and peace for all. . . ." "How indeed, after such hard years of suffering, auguish and misery, should men not rightly expect *a pro-*

---

32 Pope Pius XII, Allocution of August 5th, 1950, to the Congress of Admnistration.
33 Pope Pius XII, Allocution of August 5th, 1950, to the Congress of Admnistration.

found improvement in their conditions of existence? Hence, these *projects for reorganizing the world of work, these perspectives of structural reforms, this development of concepts of ownerships and enterprise,* sometimes envisaged in passionate haste and doctrinal confusion, but which nevertheless, must be compared with the immutable norms of reason and faith, such as the Church teaches." [34]

Pope Pius XI stated three of these structural reforms in particular in *Quadragesimo Anno*: "Wage-earners and other employees participate in the ownership or the management, or in some way share in the profits." Pius XI mentioned them as examples without passing judgment except to say that they had been tried in various ways "to the no small gain both wage-earners and of the employers." [35]

Furthermore, in the same Encyclical, the pope, after having denounced the error of "those who hold that the wage-contract is essentially unjust" added "Nevertheless, in the present state of human society, We deem it advisable that the wage-contract should, when possible, be modified somewhat by a contract of partnership."

This evolution was most carefully considered by Pius XI as his expressions "somewhat" and "when possible" indicate.

Pope Pius XII tackled the problem in his message of the 1st of September, 1944. He made clear distinction between small and medium-sized undertakings on the one hand, whose private ownership should be guaranteed, and large

---

34 Letter to M. Charles Flory, July 14th, 1945, for the Social Study Week in Toulouse
35 Pope John XXIII, in Mater et Magistra, wrote: "We regard as justifiable the desire of employees to be partners in enterprises with which they are associated and wherein they work". M.M. 91

undertakings on the other. The latter, in cases in which it should seem to be more beneficial, the pope declared *"should offer the possibility of modifying the wage-contract by a contract with society."*

In 1949, after exaggerated interpretations of the text of Pius XI, hot controversy broke out in Germany on the problem of co-partnership. Some went so far as to say that it was a natural right. Pius XII had to intervene to declare that the right of co-partnership in private enterprise is not a requirement of the natural law. And this is where he made the distinction between public and private rights.

Business enterprise does not "of its nature" come within the sphere of the state's right. The relations between the participants are therefore determined by commutative justice which governs the contracts. They are not determined "by the rules of distributive justice so that all indiscriminately—whether or not they are owners—have their right to their share of the property or at least to the profits of the enterprise." [36]

Enterprise depends on the legal order of economic life and thus on contract. Because of this the heads of large enterprises, (and we are still speaking of these), can incorporate the most varied forms of workers' participation, whether in profit-sharing, bonuses, management or partnership. And in certain cases, where the "overwhelming power of anonymous capital, if left to itself, would obviously harm the community" [37] the state can intervene to give labor the opportunity to have its say in the administration of the enterprise.

---

36 Discourse of May 7th, 1949, to the International Union of Catholic Employers
37 Letter of Msgr. Montini, September 21st, 1952, to the Italian Social Study Week.

We should note that the pope feared the incursion of organizations having no connection with the enterprise into the sphere of management and the transfer of means of production to capital-holding combines. The pope was always anxious to safeguard personal responsibility without pronouncing on the technical aspect of these reforms. He also laid down, in his concepts of man, and of the social economy, principles which called for prudent, progressive and far-reaching reforms in the structure of industry. These reforms should tend to develop and respect the personality of the workers. They should give labor greater responsibility within industry. They should give workers a more human and intelligent interest in their work so that it would become less brutalizing and more educational, and workers could use it as a means to their improvement in an economy which would, as a result, become more organic. It too often happens that the workers have the feeling of belonging to a separate world, that they are kept on the outside and that there is no place for them in the life of the national economy. It is therefore easy to see the strong appeal of the pope's call for the accession of the working class to the full exercise of its responsibilities in the national economy.

CONCLUSION

The present position of the problem of vocational organization. It must be recognized that for too long this program has been little more than a dead letter—a fine program that was never used.

But there are certain new factors which make it justifiable to say that, now at last, vocational organization has come into its own. *The first factor* is the ever-growing development of collective conventions which form the basis for vocational organization. In France, after about ten years of direct control, particularly up to 1950, during which the state rationed out raw materials and controlled credit, collective agreements were signed in 1950-1952. The first to organize themselves were the industries which were in difficulty or were undergoing a crisis and, as a result, were more aware of the need to protect the industry as a whole, e.g. textiles, transport and banks. Finally the big steel and building enterprises came in. It should also be noted that these collective agreements also settled essential questions such as the improvement of working conditions and the co-operation between employers and employees. This movement has developed particularly since 1955. From the 1st of February, 1951, to the end of 1956, 2,180 collective conventions and 4,700 wage agreements were signed. These included 85 national conventions—notably building, public services, textiles and chemical products.

The second factor is the ever-increasing interest which the large employers'· or workers' organizations take in the study of vocational organization. For a long time—from the workers' side—the Christian trade unions put forward concrete plans. What is new is the work of the French Centre of Christian Employers and of groups of technicians and of young employers who have come up with definite projects.[38]

It seems that, after years of inability to envisage any

---

38 These can be seen in the documentation of the French "Centre du Patronat Chretien." There have been similar movements in other countries, mainly in Europe.

real transformation of the present economic systems, the experts are at last tackling it.

The third factor is that Catholics have been pioneers in this development. The working out of programs and projects has been obviously inspired by Pontifical teaching on vocational organization. If Christians would decide to embark enthusiastically and soon on this course, their action would have considerable repercussions on the social life and would revolutionize the economy. While there is still time they should learn the greatness and the urgency of the task which binds them under two headings: as citizens charged with the construction and improvement of the earthly city and as Christians called to bring the world more into line with God's plan, in the name of their faith and demands of social justice and charity.

Fourth Characteristic

A DYNAMIC ECONOMY INSPIRED BY SOCIAL JUSTICE AND CHARITY

In the Encyclical, *Quadragesimo Anno*, Pius XI hailed those "who seek to restore society in the spirit of the Church, closely united in justice and charity." It is important to realize the new depth which this word "social" has in relation to individual justice and charity towards individuals.[1] Pope Pius XII, speaking to the leaders of Italian industry, told them: "You have an excellent opportunity to practice justice and charity because you can give them a social meaning."[2] And in *Mater et Magistra*, Pope John XXIII writes: "It is necessary that economic undertakings be governed by justice and charity as the principal laws of social life."[3]

---

1 Note: The Church's teaching distinguishes between justice and charity. Justice is the moral virtue which calls us to render to every man that which is due to him. Failure to practice this virtue calls for restitution. Charity towards our neighbor is the theological virtue which calls on us to love and help our fellow-men because God wills it and because this is the way in which we can show our love for Him. Failure to practice this virtue is a violation of the Divine Law and can only be pardoned by God Himself. Charity does not supersede justice; it inspires and governs it. Indeed charity obliges us to be just. An employer who thinks he can compensate for injustice towards his employees by donations to charitable causes has not understood what it is to be a Christian employer.

2 Pope Pius XII, Allocution of June 6th, 1955, to the Christian Union of Leaders of Italian Industry.

3 M.M., 39.

I. SOCIAL JUSTICE

We will consider its objective, its basis, its requirements, and what it covers.

1. *Its objective*:

It is the service of the common good. It is the duty, in justice, of each citizen to contribute to the common good of society. Social justice is a "community" affair which concerns itself with the common good and willingness to be of service. "The whole of human society," said Pius XI, "must conform to the needs of the common good, that is, to the standard of social justice." [4]

Thus, social justice is a special virtue with its own objective. It is different from "commutative" and "distributive" justice. "Commutative" justice is that which primarily affects individuals in their contractual relations with each other according to the principle of fair exchange ("I give you so that you may give me"). "Distributive" justice primarily affects the community and governs its relations with its members according to the distribution of social advantages (honors, remuneration, privileges, and assistance, etc.) and to its calls on these members.

Theologians have long defined "legal" justice which is concerned with law, as the virtue which guides legislators to make laws in the interests of the common good and which also obliges citizens to obey such laws.

Social justice coincides with legal justice when it is manifest in social laws made by the state for the common

---

4 Quadragesimo Anno.

good. But it is wider and more extensive than legal justice in so far as it aims at the creation of social order which requires the co-operation not only of the legislator but of all citizens and institutions.

Social justice is concerned with the relations of citizens with the common good, both in their duties and rights. It it invoked in two ways, i.e. the relation of the community to the citizens and vice versa. On the one hand it demands respect for the natural *rights* of the members of the community, so that they may be able to fulfil their *duties* and functions in society.[5] On the other hand it is the virtue which influences citizens to render to society that which they owe it, so that society may be able to fulfil its mission towards the common good by giving everyone what he requires to develop his personality and fulfil his social function.

2. *The basis of social justice.*

The elements of social justice are: the social nature of man, the organic concept of society and the social end of material goods.

The first element of social justice is in *the social nature of man* in the sense that the individual can live and develop fully only in a society which provides all that is necessary for the physical, intellectual and moral life of man. Now there are several social categories which are deprived in some degree of this natural right. It is towards these categories which are in need and which have the right to live in a more human manner that social justice should first of all be directed. The duty arises from the nature which all men share in common

---

5 Pope Pius XI, defined social justice in the Encyclical, Quadragesimo Anno.

and from the responsibilities which all citizens share, as members of society, towards their fellow-members who are deprived of the practical use of their natural rights in society.

The second element is the *organic concept of society*. Society is not a conglomeration of individuals thrown to-gether—it is a living body whose members should help each other so that all can effectively take part in the life of the human community.[6]

The third element is *the social end of material goods*, so that they can serve the needs of all according to the principles of a more just distribution of wealth.

To sum up, what the Church demands by social justice is "a just and proper sharing by all in the wealth of the nation." [7] "It is important to give everyone what he is entitled to and to bring back the distribution of the resources of this world to the norms of social justice." [8]

3. *The requirements of social justice.*

These are expressed by the creation of a judicial and social order destined to replace the economic life under the law of a just and effective guiding principle. Class-warfare, or abso-lutely free competition, or an economic dictatorship (all forces which have withdrawn from the moral law) cannot ensure a well-ordered economic system. "More lofty and noble principles must therefore be sought in order to control this dictatorship sternly and uncompromisingly; to wit, social justice and social charity. To that end all institutions of public

---

6 Cfr. M.M., 219.
7 Pope Pius XII, Whitsun 1943, Discourse to workers on social problems.
8 Quadragesimo Anno.

and social life must be imbued with the spirit of justice, which must be truly operative, must build up a juridical and social order pervading the whole economic regime."[9]

In the same way Pius XII demanded that we should "fully co-operate in the advent of a public order which realizes, to the greatest possible degree, a sound and social justice." [10] It is not a question of a few reforms here and there but of a complete transformation of society.

Social justice is very demanding in its requirements. It embraces all the other virtues to bring about its objective, which is the common good. The repercussion on the lives of individuals and of society would be enormous if everybody were to consider the common good instead of purely selfish interests, to develop a social sense and bear in mind the consequences of his actions on others. As an example, take the virtue of prudence; the driver of a car can practise it to save himself or avoid prosecution. How different would be his driving were he to apply prudence in the name of social justice and positively co-operate in the common good by respecting the rules of the road irrespective of the fear of a penalty!

Take another example; temperance. Everyone can deny himself certain alcoholic drinks to safeguard his personal health. It is quite another thing to consider alcoholism as a grave social evil and fight against it in the name of social justice.

This could be continued for every virtue; by passing from an individualistic to a community concept, which

---

9 Pope Pius XI, Quadragesimo Anno.
10 Pope Pius XII, Allocution to the Sacred College of Cardinals, June 2nd, 1947.

ensures the idea of social justice, we bring about results which are beneficial to all.

4. *The scope of social justice.*

Social justice applies wherever there is a question of the common good. Its domain is universal.

In particular, social justice arises in relations between workers and the community as a whole to complete whatever is due to the worker in strict "commutative" justice by the employer. Problems of family allowances, social insurance, protection and insurance against accidents, unemployment, sickness, disability, old age (homes and pensions) and, in a general way, vocational organization and collective agreements should all be resolved and balance maintained between wages and prices.

Social justice requires the setting up of institutions and organizations which will allow workers and citizens to bring about reforms which would be beyond them as individuals.

Social justice overflows the national framework more and more, and now extends to relations between nations. It imposes on them the duty of co-operating to solve social problems. That is why Pius XII demanded, as we saw earlier, the universal co-operation of peoples and states to remedy the evil of unemployment. Each should bring its contribution according to its resources of raw materials, capital and manpower.[11] Socal justice applies to the use of the different resources of the world.

---

11 Pope Pius XII, Allocution of June 3rd, 1950, to the International Congress of Social Studies at the University of Fribourg.

II. Social Charity

After showing the necessity of the order of social justice Pius XI continued in *Quadragesimo Anno*: "Social charity should be, as it were, the soul of this order, an order which the state must actively defend and vindicate." Too many Christians still do not know that charity is thus presented to them in a new dimension and that individual charity no longer suffices. There must be a social charity concerned with people but not just as separate individuals.

This virtue, still little studied by theologians and too little known by Christians on the whole, possesses a particular effectiveness in promoting social progress and in transforming temporal institutions. It inspires specialized Catholic Action to press its members to relieve the social tension between the classes and to change living conditions, outlook and customs and, indirectly, institutions. Thus the whole environment makes it possible to live a Christian life worthy of a son of God, and, opening to the redeeming grace of Jesus Christ and the Church's mediation, it directs itself towards the ideal of the restoration of all things in Christ.[12]

Charity which concerns itself with the common good.

Like social justice, by which it is inspired, social charity disposes men to seek together the common good of society but its influence goes further into the very hearts of men. It first of all gives Christians new motives for social action, then a new objective for such action and, finally, the inspiration of a new principle.

---

12 Cfr. M.M., 6.

a) *new motives*: These actions concerned with the common good are brought about by social charity and no longer in the name of the claims of justice nor under the compulsion of a rigid state law but *through love*—love of God and men. Men are no longer considered individually but are united in *society*, living in a *social body*. Social charity applies to life in a community.

b) *a new objective*: This temporal common good is pursued by social charity so that it may be directed to the *eternal good* and *destiny of man*. In other words social charity seeks a social order more in conformity with God's plan, more worthy of mankind redeemed and better able to ensure the human and supernatural fruition of the Redemption. It tries to bring about here on earth, an order of social relations between men which will prefigure the eternal city where all men will love each other in God.

c) *a new principle*: This principle *is divine*. It is that of the divine life of charity and grace which springs from the Heart of Jesus Christ, Head of the Mystical Body, and which is spread to the members of that Body by the Holy Spirit, the soul of the Church. Through this life and all the virtues it enkindles, the Church, which is the Mystical Body, inspires mankind. It is by the Church's mediation that the fruitfulness of this life is transferred to the social body and it is through the conscience of the complete man (formed by her) that the Church ceaselessly works to establish the solid foundations of society.

"Considered from this point of view, one can say that the Church is the society of those who, under the supernatural influence of grace, in the perfection of their personal dignity as sons of God and in the harmonious development of all human dispositions and energies, build the powerful framework of the human community." [13]

We can call it a dynamic economy in the sense that the vital principles of social justice and charity are constant stimulants to combat stagnation, laissez-faire and conservatism hardened into the acceptance and maintenance of a state of social injustice. They press lay Christians, who follow the logic of their faith, to continually look for social progress and human betterment. These virtues impose a duty to refuse to be part of a social system which is contrary to God's will for the development of men and the organization of society in justice and charity.

---

13 Pope Pius XII, Allocution to the Consistory, February 20th, 1946.

Fifth Characteristic

AN ECONOMY SUBORDINATE TO THE MORAL LAW

The fifth characteristic of the social economy gives Christian thought a particular slant which makes it different from other concepts of economy; it is the synthesis of the preceding characteristic.

The Church's social teaching does not accept the modern widespread thesis that the economy is outside the moral law. Of course the economy has its own laws and methods. The two domains are distinct but not separate. For, says Pius XII, "complete separation has no meaning in life, which is always a synthesis, since the sole subject of all kind of activity is the same man whose free and conscious actions cannot escape the moral law." [1] And John XXIII says: "Man is composed not merely of body, but of soul as well, and endowed with reason and freedom. Now such a composite being absolutely requires a moral law rooted in religion, which, far better than any external force or advantage, can contribute to the resolution of problems affecting the lives of individual citizens or groups of citizens." [2]

The subject concerned in the economy is man and not the *homo economicus* which economic schools have built up out of an abstract idea; it is the whole man, of flesh and blood, the human person with his freedom and conscience,

---

[1] Pope Pius XII, Message on the Family, March 23rd, 1952.
[2] M.M., 208.

who is subject to the moral law in all that he does. It must be added that it is also man, the sinner, with his concupiscence, egoism and greed. This being so "theoretical autonomism as regards the moral law becomes, in fact, rebellion against the moral law." [3]

This is so true that the releasing of the economy from the moral law, since the beginning of Liberalism in the last century down to our own day, has resulted in a materialistic and soulless technical civilization. It has caused terrible suffering and cruel anomalies.

We want to underline two aspects of the problem:

1) The principle of the subordination of the economy to the moral law enlightens the judgment which Christians should make on the different economies of capitalistic liberalism and Marxist communism.

2) The final solution of economic problems is found not only in the transformation of institutions but in the restoration of the moral law.

I. JUDGMENT ON DIFFERENT ECONOMIES NOT IN ACCORD WITH THE MORAL LAW

It would be quite impossible to pass judgment on every type of economy, so we will select two principal ones: liberal capitalism and Marxist communism. [4] The judgment

---

3 Pope Pius XII, Message on the Family, March 23rd, 1952.
4 We choose these two systems because they have been integrally applied and their principles are clear-cut. As regards socialism, we consider Marxist socialism on the Marxist principles on which it is based. But there are many kinds of socialism and it is impossible to make a study of each type here.

of the Church's social teaching is concerned only with their disregard for the moral law. This affords the means of showing why the social teaching lays such stress on the subordination of the moral law.

1. *Economic Liberalism*

Economic liberalism ignores and breaks the moral law in several ways:

1) in its *aim*. According to economic liberalism the most important aim of the economy is to produce more and more in order to have the greatest possible wealth and material prosperity.

Naturally the Church's social teaching does not underestimate the necessity for increased productivity as a condition for the temporal common good. But it also teaches that there is a hierarchy of values. The supreme value here below is neither the economic life nor material prosperity. It is man himself. Everything else should be subordinate to him, including economic life.

Liberalism essentially has a concept of man and the social economy which is in conflict with this Christian concept.

2) in the *motivation* of economic activity—for liberalism—personal interest is the rule. Let everyone follow his own interests in perfect freedom and the general interest will be realized!

The Church's social teaching allows personal interest, profit and the honest growth of individual and family property. She sees them as a stimulus to man to fulfil his duty, as necessary for economic progress and as a return for services rendered. But the Church knows man and his deeply-rooted selfishness, the fruit of original sin; she knows that his passions are an obstacle to clear vision and the pursuit of the common good. She teaches that the common good will not be assured by giving full rein to individual freedom but that the moral law, which calls for justice and charity, must be obeyed.

3) in the *composition* of economic life; liberalism demands the complete liberty of the producer and free competition for the maximum profit. Thus, there is no room for economic and social groups such as vocational organizations or unions, which would limit or curtail the liberty of individuals.

Results. The door is open to all kinds of abuses in the exploitation of the worker.

Individualism is unleashed in business relations and bitter trade war, totally disregarding justice and charity, ensues between competitors.[5]

Mammon is worshipped, the common good is systematically ignored and human values and God's plan are contradicted.

Such habitual conduct dulls the conscience. The producers, slaves of liberalism, become hard and insensitive to the sufferings and misery of men. Finally it makes the economy materialistic and pagan—the very opposite to the Christian concept of the social economy.

Liberal Capitalism.

The results mentioned above show why the popes condemned liberal capitalism so severely.

---

5 Cfr. M.M., 36.

Leo XIII—end of nineteenth century (1891)—This was the era of free competition. The pursuit of the maximum profit led the heads of industry to cut their prices and thus lower the conditions of the workers in order to beat their competitors.

In the Encyclical *Rerum Novarum,* Leo XIII denounced the low wages which the isolated and defenseless workers had to accept "at the mercy of inhuman masters and the greed of unbridled competition." The pope also condemned the abuses in the working conditions of women and children who were hired because they could be paid less. Finally, the pope denounced the overlong working hours and the absence of decent facilities and weekly day of rest.

This amoral system, which caused so many evils, was defined by Leo XIII by this striking contrast: on one side a concentration of wealth and the means of production in the hands of a few, and, on the other, the mass of the proletariat in poverty and under an almost servile yoke.

Pius XI—Forty years later. The liberal era was followed by an era of supercapitalism, "a veritable economic dictatorship" as the pope called it in the Encyclical, *Quadragesimo Anno.* This is the age of big deals and mergers, cartels and trusts. "In our days not only wealth is accumulated, but immense power and despotic economic domination are concentrated in the hands of a few, who for the most part are not the owners, but only the trustees and directors of invested funds, which they administer at their own good pleasure."

Pius XI forcefully condemned the economic and social disorders of such a system and its inhuman character. *The whole economic life had become terribly hard, implacable and cruel.* There was "an unquenchable thirst for riches ..." "hardened against the stings of conscience." Many have been impelled "to break the law of God and trample on the rights of their neighbor."

But what is the cause of these disorders? They are due to the *alienation of economic science from the moral law.*[6]

Considered in the abstract, this capitalist system is not bad in itself, declared Pius XI, but it has been vitiated, "But it violates right order whenever capital employs the worker or the proletariat with a view and on such terms as to direct business and economic activity entirely at its own arbitrary will and its own advantage, without any regard to the human dignity of the workers, the social character of the economic regime, social justice and the common good."

In 1937, in the Encyclical, *Divini Redemptoris,* where he states that "liberalism opened up the way for Communism," Pius XI condensed all his teaching of *Qudragesimo Anno.* He has "shown the means of saving the modern world from the misery into which a moral liberalism has plunged us." He adds, in addressing the employers, that they carry "the heavy inheritance of an *unjust economic system which has carried on its ravages throughout several generations."* And in *Mater et Magistra,* Pope John XXIII states: "If the organization and structure of economic life be such that the human dignity of workers is compromised, or their sense of responsibility is weakened, or their freedom of action is removed, then we judge such an economic order to be unjust, even

---

6 Pope Pius XI, Quadragesimo Anno: "For at the time when the new economic order was beginning, the doctrines of rationalism had already taken firm hold of large numbers, and an economic science alien to the moral law quickly arose and consequently free rein was given to man's inordinate desires."

though it produces a vast amount of goods, whose distribution conforms to the norms of justice and equity." [7]

Naturally the Church's enemies continue to accuse her of never denouncing the economic system of liberal capitalism and even of being subject to it. The popes indignantly refuted this accusation which they called a "calumny". A calumny indeed since the texts are there, clear, explicit and indisputable. What is true, unfortunately, is that too many leaders of industry chose to ignore them. Pius XI condemned this attitude severely.

Pius XII. We have already quoted from the great war-time messages of Pius XII—that of Christmas, 1942, condemning a social system opposed to God's order and that of September, 1944, condemning, as contrary to the natural law, a system which arrogates to itself an unlimited right of ownership without any reference to the common good.

Finally, in his Discourse for the Tenth Anniversary of the Christian Association of Italian Workers, May 1st, 1955, Pius XII energetically protested against "the atrocious calumny that 'the Church is allied to capitalism against the workers'" and the pope recalled his Christmas Message of 1942.

To sum up, the Church's teaching, judging the capitalist system with reference to the moral law, condemns it not in its nature (for it recognizes the lawfulness of income and profit once justice is respected), but for what it in fact does and practices. It is not only particular abuses and errors that are condemned but the "social system" itself where it is based on a concept of private ownership opposed to the community

---

7 M.M., 83.

end assigned by God to the goods of the earth. Such a concept would ignore the common good and condemn the worker "to a dependence, to an economic servitude irreconcilable with the rights of the person" [8] and become "a power directed to the exploitation of the work of others." [9]

2. *Communism*

The Church's social teaching condemns communism for different reasons: 1) Because it is essentially *materialistic, atheistic and anti-Christian*. The concept it presents of man, life and society is contrary to Christian truth. The true destiny of man is ignored. Marxist Communism considers everything as depending on matter. For it neither the soul, nor God, exist. Society is considered as being created only for material prosperity. Communism denies that man's life has any sacred or spiritual character.[10]

Communism sees religion as an obstacle to the liberation of man. Marx wanted a liberation which would not only free man socially from capitalism but also, spiritually, from God and religion. For him religion was the cause of fundamental alienation of man. (Marx considered that religion directed man from his vital role in the dialectic and thus distorted his true mission).

Communism has always and everywhere fought against religion and organized violent persecutions against the Church in the countries where it is master.

2) Because Communism ignores the *rights of the human person* and dignity of his freedom. It delivers him defense-

---

8 Christmas Message, 1942.
9 Christmas Message, 1941.
10 Pope Pius XI, Encyclical, Divini Redemptoris.

less to the Communist State in absolute submission in the name of an inhuman totalitarianism which makes man a slave to production. That is why Pius XII can say that he condemned communism as *a social system because of Christian teaching.*[11]

3) Because it *refuses to submit to a higher authority* than that of the individual,—to the authority of the moral law, natural right and God, the Sovereign Creator, Lawgiver and Judge.

4) Because it preaches *class-warfare* as an inescapable law of history and duty which binds the workers, in violation of the law of universal charity.

Experience now shows how right the Church was to use these reasons, of a doctrinal nature, to denounce the dangers of Communism.

Communism was applied in soviet Russia under Stalin's dictatorship. It is not a question of just a brief interlude, for Stalin was head of the party and of the country for thirty years. Neither is it a question of stories invented by the enemies of Communism, for these revelations were made by Khrushchev himself, as Secretary General of the Communist Party, at the Twentieth Congress of the Communist Party of the Soviet Union, February 25th, 1956, in a supposedly confidential report.[12]

What then do we learn from this document? It described

---

11 Pope Pius XII, Christmas Message, 1955.
12 The report ends with these words: "No word of this matter should leak to the outside world; the press particularly should not be informed. That is why we are considering it here, in secret session. There is a limit to everything and there is no reason why we should furnish our enemies with ammunition. There is no need to wash dirty linen in public." But the report was divulged.

in sobering terms the implacable dictatorship which Stalin wielded over Soviet Russia, particularly since 1929 until his death.

Massive repressions were carried out by government machinery. There were numerous arrests of officials of the party, of the Soviets, and the army, often on warrants of arrest issued by Stalin himself in his arbitrary power, equipped with all the trappings of law and falsified documents.[13] "Physical pressure and torture" were applied "to deprive the accused of his faculties and judgment and take away his human dignity. That is how the 'confessions' were obtained." [14]

Then there were the mass deportations of millions of people, "entire populations" says the report, and executions without trial.

The Communists, embarrassed by these revelations about facts which they would have preferred kept secret, tried, not to justify them, because they knew they could not, but to discount this testimony by declaring that, even if Stalin had committed certain "errors," he had also rendered immense services to the working-class and established great industries in his country for the material good of the people.

No one can deny that there has been progress in Russia in the technical and material sectors of the national economy. We are only dealing here with the moral plane and it must therefore be stated that Stalin not only committed "errors" but vertitable *crimes* which this report even severely con-

---

13 The doctors' plot, says the report, was "a pure invention from beginning to end."

14 This part of the report confirms the judgment of world opinion on those who obtained false confessions from unfortunate victims, not only in Russia but in other countries subject to her yoke.

demns. But there is more to it than that and the lesson is surely that if Stalin committed so many crimes over such a long period it is precisely because he deliberately ignored and openly violated all the rules of a universal moral law greater than the economy. *He did not recognize any authority other than himself—no moral law, no natural right, nor God.* He was the absolute master and, says the report, he made of himself "a superman, endowed with supernatural (sic) powers, equal to God."

Here an objection is offered: "but then the very interest of the party to which he was sincerely attached should have sufficed to stop him in his path."

The manner of the reply in the report is yet more striking. "In acting as he did, Stalin was convinced that he acted in the interests of the working-class, in the interests of the people, for the victory of socialism and of communism."—And the report ended on this note: *"This is where the tragedy lies."*

This is indeed where the tragedy of Communist morality lies. According to it an act is not judged good because it conforms to an objective moral law; it is judged good because it is in the interests of the party and of Communism. Stalin logically applied the principle of Communist morality—once he felt he was acting in the interests of the party and for the victory of Socialism there was nothing to make him pause in his criminal work. Here indeed the end was held to justify the means.

Would collective direction have prevented such folly? In collective or personal dictatorship the danger is the same once the party interest is placed above all moral rules. For since Stalin has died, the interest of the party has sent military divisions and tanks to massacre the populations of

Berlin, Poznan and Budapest and the collective administration did not even demur.

There remains a final moral lesson to be gained from the experience of Stalin. According to Communism, man is not the source of evil—this comes only from the structure of capitalism. As soon as these have been destroyed the Communist will make a "new man" and a true humanism will be possible.

We can study this claim in relation to Stalin's regime which took place under unique conditions. Starting from a certain period when he had liquidated all his opponents and consolidated his party,[15] he was the uncontested head of Communism in his country. He was the arbiter of doctrine, of orthodoxy. By his position and temperament he was free from the slightest "pernicious" influence of the capitalist system.

But what does the report show? A man who was excessively brutal, capricious, autocratic in the extreme and who demanded absolute submission under pain of moral and physical annihilation and who was distrustful and unhealthily suspicious. After the war, his mania for persecution reached unbelievable proportions. Fired with limitless vanity, he re-wrote eulogies in his honor to attribute everyone else's achievements and genius to himself. He raised statues to himself when alive. Convinced that he never made a mistake, he supposed himself to be infallible, knowing everything and capable of doing everything.

If we mention these traits of Stalin in the terms of the

---

15 "Stalin had recourse to extreme methods and massive oppressions even when the Revolution had succeeded, when the Soviet State had been consolidated and when the exploiters had been liquidated...." (Report).

report it is because we touch here on one of the most irredeemable weaknesses of Communism. Since it denies the existence of evil in man's sin it is powerless to achieve the true remedy for such evil. . . . Of course economic structures have a powerful influence on man's social condition and we have already analyzed the structures of the capitalist system in its serious attacks on the human person. But even if the structures of society were changed, as long as man keeps his sin, pride, ambition, jealousy and egoism there will be neither peace nor true happiness on earth. Doubtless Communism can inspire generous and even heroic sacrifices in its convinced militants for a certain time. But it is powerless to purify and liberate man from his evil tendencies, selfish instincts and the slavery of his passions. For that a redeemer is needed.

Stalin's conduct proved that, even in the highest position in the party, there remains sinful man and, in order to overcome himself, he needs a morality which is greater than himself.

II. REFORMS IN PRACTICE

The Church's social doctrine teaches that it is not sufficient to transform the structures of society—it is necessary to have reform in practice.

Revolution, reform or transformation?

Here the question is raised: "Is the Church for or against the social revolution? If she is against it, will she be satisfied with mere reforms?"

The Church's social teaching has never favored the social revolution for several reasons:

First of all this term "social revolution" implies violent disruptions, serious and unjust attacks on people and property, the kindling of passion and hatred, and the accumulation of disorder and ruin which remain for years.

Furthermore, those who have the revolution as their objective are inclined to "reject with understandable, but unreasonable and unjustifiable impatience, truly organic reforms."[16] It seems to them that all social reform which might improve the worker's lot only consolidates the present system and postpones the revolution. Such an attitude may well become an obstacle to any immediate social progress.

Finally, the revolution considered as an objective, is too often used as an excuse to avoid doing something constructive to transform society. How many of those who are revolutionaries in spirit do not know what they would substitute for the system they want to overthrow or, if they do know, it is a dream of a system in which the working class would remain bound and enslaved to a state capitalism which would subjugate the whole world and transform labor into an enormous machine.[17]

The social doctrine of the Church declares itself for "a progressive and prudent evolution, courageous and in conformity with nature, enlightened and guided by the holy Christian laws of justice and equity."[18]

But we must not think that it is only a question of a little touching up here and there and a few reforms which

---

16 Pope Pius XII, Message of September 1st, 1944.
17 Pope Pius XII, Allocution to Italian workers, June 13th, 1943.
18 Quadragesimo Anno.

do not go to the root of the problem. On the contrary, the Church's social teaching aims at a complete transformation of society in its entire structure, of the social system and the social economy. It tends towards a radical renewal not only in institutions but—and this is how it differs from many reforms which are merely economic in objective—in the minds and hearts of men. Pius XI called for the complete *renewal* of the Christian spirit from which so many people engaged in industry have at times lamentably departed." [19] In the midst of war, Pius XII analyzed "the desire for *a new order*" and discerned a clear vision of the deficiencies of the present order and a deep desire for an order which would guarantee the juridical rules of national and international life.[20] He sought a new era for the "profound renewal and the complete reorganization of the world." [21] A few years later he called for "a profound and solid reconstruction of society," [22] *a new world,* a world ordered in its juridical structure, a more equitable and healthy world in which men would devote themselves to suppressing injustice and pursue motives of fraternal reconciliation rather than sources of discord or rancour." [23]

To this work, which Pius XII described as the *re-education of mankind* which should be spiritual and religious above all, starting with Christ as its prerequisite foundation, realized by justice and crowned by charity,[24] the Church brings the loyal and powerful support of her social teaching

---

19 Quadragesimo Anno.
20 Radio Message, December 24th, 1940.
21 Message, December 25th, 1944.
22 Letter of July 14th, 1945, to M. Charles Flory.
23 Pope Pius XII, Letter to the French Hierarchy, January 8th, 1945.
24 Pope Pius XII, Encyclical Summi Pontificatus, October 20th, 1939.

to enlighten men's minds and permeate their will, conscience and heart, "to bring man to obey the dictates of duty, to master the passions, to love God and his neighbor with a particular and sovereign charity and to overcome courageously all the obstacles which he meets in the path of virtue.[25] The instruments at the Church's disposal to reach souls—the sacraments, grace, the sacrifice of the Mass and the guidance of the Hierarchy—have been given to her by Jesus Christ Himself.

---

25 Pope Leo XII, Rerum Novarum.

CONCLUSION

The fundamental principles of the Church's social teaching are nothing but the expression of the natural law and reason, enlightened by Revelation.[1]

1) To render to the *human person* his dignity, his true freedom and his rights. The social forms which make possible and guarantee full personal responsibility in the temporal as well as in the eternal order must be encouraged by lawful means and in all spheres of life.

2) To defend, protect and restore *the family* in its economic, spiritual, moral and legal unity. To procure for it living-space, leisure and a home not too far from the place of work so that it can fulfil its mission to transmit new life, raise children and provide a family life which is both materially and spiritually good.

3) To give *work* the place in society marked out for it by God, to respect its dignity "as the indispensable means of conquering the world, the means designed by God for His glory" (Pius XII), the means of personal fulfilment and union between men. The pain and burden which it carries as a result of orginal sin does not destroy the dignity of work. But this dignity itself and the restoration of all things in Christ demand vigorous social action in the interests of the masses.

---

1 Message of Pope Pius XII, December 24th, 1942.

4) *To ensure that the workers and their families have*:

a) *living and working conditions* (wages, housing, private ownership) which redress injustice and render possible a better and more human life and security in the respect due to the dignity of the worker; —b) the opportunity for a human *culture*; —c) the place which the workers should hold *in the nation* side by side with the other classes so that they may "take their responsibility in the administration of the whole economy of the country." [2] The aspirations of the workers coincide to a remarkable extent with the changes envisaged in the Church's social teaching.

5) To tend to *unify society* with loyal co-operation between different classes and professions by setting up a vocational organization calculated to further the common good of the vocational group by more human, more just and more fraternal relations.

6) To develop a sense of the *common good* as a principle of unity by fighting against "the unbridled egoism which is the shame and great sin of our age." [3] Then to encourage the extension of social justice and charity to institutions and laws, that they may serve the human person and its dignity. To bring about a more equitable distribution of wealth and the national income in order to raise the standard of living of the less favored classes.

7) To promote a true conception of *the State*. "No social institution, other than the family, is so vital and essential as the state. Its roots are in the order of creation and it is

---

2 Pope Pius XII, Allocution to the Catholic Association of Italian workers, June 29th, 1948.
3 Pope Pius XI, Quadragesimo Anno.

itself one of the constituent elements of the natural law." [4]
The state has the function of encouraging, helping and
promoting the co-operation of all for the good of the whole
community, neither absorbing the individual nor the family
but, on the contrary, protecting their rights and freedoms,
particularly if they are threatened.[5] The state has the noble
mission of being the guardian of rights of which it is not the
origin. As it is the first servant and administrator of the common good, it must be the first to respect it. Of course the complexity, extent and ramifications of national and international
life today have considerably enlarged its sphere of action.
This is but an added reason why the state should not abuse
its powers or become totalitarian but should retain a true
idea of its role and function.

8) *To correlate the juridical and moral orders.* Every man
has the right to juridical security and this must not be
threatened by arbitrary acts of the legislature, of the police
or of the judiciary yielding to pressures of power or party.
What is legal is not necessarily right—a law is not just merely
because it has been voted by a parliament. The Creator has
given a criterion to men's hearts to judge whether a law is
just or not and this is the natural law, the light of reason
based on the true nature of man and things and expressly
confirmed by Revelation.

9) *To make the masses, an amorphous multitude of individuals, into true people.*
The masses are not a people.[6] The masses are subject to
external forces and are led without knowing where they go.

---

4 Pope Pius XII, Allocution to the Congress of Administration, August 5th,1950.
5 Cfr. M.M., 20.
6 Pope Pius XII, Message of December 24th, 1944.

A people lives from the fullness of the life of men who compose it. In a nation every citizen, in his own place, is a free person, cognizant of his dignity, responsibilities, convictions, rights and duties and mindful of the freedom and responsibilities of others.

In a true democracy the citizens have rights which authority should respect—the right to a personal opinion on the rights and duties which are imposed upon them, the right to be consulted and to have their opinion put into effect in a manner consistent with the common good. "The state should be the organic and organizing unity of true people." (Pius XII)

10. There can be no real social progress or civilization without *reference to God and a return to the Gospel of Jesus Christ* as taught by the Church.[7] The Church's social teaching recalls that, above and beyond the efforts of men or peoples or their governments to build the earthly city, there is the law of God and Gospel to teach them the absolute order of beings and their purposes, the true hierarchy of values, an ideal of truth, justice and liberty and the need for all to share more justly in the world's goods, whether material, cultural or social. The Church's social teaching denounces the scandal of those Christians who outwardly practise their religion but do not yet understand that their salvation will depend on the way in which they practise justice and charity in their professional and social life. It imposes on Christians the duty of taking part in social and political developments which work for the transformation of the earthly city. It shows them the principles which should guide their action,

---

7 Cfr. M.M., 215.

the errors to be avoided, the spirit which should inspire them and the nobility and urgency of this social mission.

THE EXTENT OF THE SOCIAL TEACHING

Objection. Faced with this noble ideal there are already some who object: "All this is certainly very fine. But this ideal is so abstract, far-away and so completely in opposition to the whole structure of economic society and the complexity of the modern world that it is impossible to see how it could enlighten and guide Christians who are in the thick of the fight against the injustices of social life today."

The Church is the first to recognize that this ideal is in strong contrast to the world around us as we see it. That is why she makes bold to declare that there must be *"a complete reorganization and a profound renewal of the world."* (Pius XII)

Further, if we want to understand the grave reasons for the popes' insistence on the pressing necessity and binding character of the Church's social teaching, the ideal must be seen in all its dimensions and in the full extent of its objective. "The whole world must be re-made from its very foundations. From being inhuman it must be made human, from being human it must be made divine, that is to say, according to the Heart of God." [8] In addition we have seen how the popes have proclaimed that the structures of economic life are too often inhuman and that they crush the human person. "The whole of economic life has become horribly harsh, implacable and cruel." Who said that?—Pope

---

8 Pope Pius XII, Radio Message, February 10, 1952.

Pius XI.[9] And again: "Social life seems to have become an enigma and an inextricable tangle;" "Society is like a gigantic machine of which man is no longer the master and which he even fears." These were the words of Pius XII.[10]

Furthermore, no one knows better than the Church that the task of "rebuilding a new world according to justice and love" [11] is hard and difficult because, apart from the opposition of established interests, she foresees the resistance that will come from human weaknesses like sin, selfishness, hard hearts and cowardice. The Church knows that much courage, initiative enterprise and clear thinking will be necessary for this battle. Pius XII called for clear vision, devotion, courage, inventive genius and fraternal charity in all right and honest hearts, to determine in what way and to what extent the Christian spirit will succeed in maintaining and consolidating the enormous work of the restoration of social, economic and international life on a plane reconcilable with the religious and moral content of Christian civilization.[12]

And again, addressing the Roman aristocracy: "Your role presupposes much study, much work, much abnegation and above all, much love." [13] In the same discourse the pope denounced the enemies of the task of construction; the desertion of those who held themselves aloof, the abstention of the sullen or disgruntled man who, discontented or discouraged, makes no use of his qualities and energies, does not take part in any of the activities of his country or of his time, but withdraws into his shell. . .the abstention of indolent and passive indifference. . .the unconcern in the face of ruin which

9 Pope Pius XI, Encyclical, Quadragesimo Anno.
10 Pope Pius XII, February 20th, 1946.
11 Pope Pius XII, October 20th, 1939.
12 Pope Pius XII, Message of September 1st, 1944.
13 Pope Pius XII, Discourse of February 8th, 1947.

threatens one's own brothers and people. This abstention is never neutral, as those who indulge in it claim; "it is" says the pope, "whether we wish it or not an accessory."

Finally, Pope John XXIII wrote: "Principles of this kind must not only be known and understood, but also applied to those systems and methods, which the various situations of time or place either suggest or require. This is indeed a difficult, though lofty, task. Toward its fulfillment we exhort not only our brothers and sons everywhere, but all men of good will." [14]

These are the moral qualities required from men of action of all walks of life for this work of reconstruction.

"The co-operation of men of learning and of science, of economists, sociologists, and specialists with the Church, is required if she is to apply her teaching to our epoch," They should keep the Hierarchy informed of the technical manner in which economic and social problems arise today, of the present state of economics and sociology and the analysis of economic structures which weigh so heavily on moral, family and human life and which change remarkably quickly, particularly under the effects of the U.N.O. and its agencies and of the assistance given by better-off nations to under-developed areas.

A Final Objection

There remains one last, important objection to be answered. Some will say: "Of course we know the great Papal Encyclicals on the social teaching of the Church. But how many of the texts you have quoted are extracts from radio-

---

14 M.M., 221.

messages or allocutions of Pope Pius XII. Now, even if we can accept that the Encyclicals have real authority, it does not necessarily follow—no matter how interesting these interventions may be—that we accept allocutions to pilgrims or to groups with common interest like cyclists or tobacco planters etc. as having the same authority."

Reply—The Authority of Papal Documents.

There are several misapprehensions in this oft-repeated objection. In briefly explaining the following doctrinal points it will be easier to see the position of the social teaching of the Church and the authority with which the different papal documents are to be regarded by the faithful.[15]

The living Magisterium of the Church exercises its teaching mission in two ways: 1) by extraordinary means; 2) by ordinary means.

1) *By extraordinary means*: in a solemn and infallible judgement on a subject relating to faith and morals, by an Ecumenical Council (the Sovereign Pontiff with the entire Episcopal College in communion with him)—or by the pope speaking *ex cathedra*, i.e. as Pastor and Teacher of all Christians, by virtue of his supreme apostolic authority, and defining that a doctrine of faith or morals should be held by the Universal Church.

Such judgment is infallible. Such a doctrine becomes dogma and he who rejects it is a heretic.

---

15 The "Revue Thomiste" (July-September 1956). An article on "Le magistere ordinaire du Souverain Pontife."

Because of the solemn character of this exceptional manner of teaching, many Christians are tempted to consider it as the only rule of faith. This is a grave error which would considerably reduce the domain of the Church's authority; for such extraordinary intervention is quite exceptional (two or three times in a century) and is made only under particular conditions. Furthermore, a papal pronouncement ought to be obeyed not only because it is infallible but because it is, to an extent which can be determined, the pronouncement of the Head of the Church, the Teacher and Pastor of the Universal Church, to which Jesus Christ has promised (in addition to the extraordinary and infallible help of the Holy Spirit in certain grave but rare circumstances) a continuing help for all time. "And behold I am with you all through the days that are coming, until the consummation of the world." (Mat. XXVIII. 20)

2) *By ordinary means.* The encyclicals, allocutions and letters, which Pius XII described as the documents in which the social teaching of the Church was to be mainly found, are the normal channels of the ordinary magisterium. This is concerned not only with an isolated proposition of faith but with the whole of the living deposit of truths to be taught. This ordinary and universal magisterium is made up of the unanimous teaching of the episcopal body in communion with the pope, each bishop in his diocese and the pope for the Universal Church, all teaching the truth. It is the normal process of Tradition.

Now there is here a true rule of faith which requires the adherence of the faithful who can advance from simple respect to a true act of faith. The teaching of the ordinary magisterium can also be infallible; the pope could choose to give a solemn definition by means of an Encyclical or even a radio message. Apart from these cases where infallibility may be exercised, the ordinary magisterium is the *authentic* teaching which is binding on the faithful.

The Attitude of the faithful to the Teaching of the Ordinary Magisterium.

1) The most important thing is that faithful and clergy should have a particularly respectful, prudent, proper and receptive attitude towards any pronouncement of the pope. The Head of the Church has the right to expect a responsive attitude. The truly faithful will immediately go further and put themselves in a general disposition of faith towards the mystery of the Church, believing that Jesus Christ invisibly guides His Church by the Holy Spirit and visibly by the Supreme Pontiff of the Universal Church, the Head and Teacher, the Pastor of all the Faithful. The Encyclical, *Humani Generis* laid down that the words of the Gospel, "He who listens to you listens to me," also apply to whatever is taught by the ordinary magisterium.

2) Those priests or layfolk who then want to make an analysis of the document will seek to ascertain the degree of authority given by the pope to his intervention and the obedience it calls for.

What is important in this aim is to discover to what extent the pope wishes to employ his authority in the document. Did he merely want to sound a warning or to give advice? Did he want to indicate a positive direction or give a certain interpretation? Did he want to expound a doctrine in a positive manner or to settle a controversy, or to declare that such a matter was no longer to be considered an open question between theologians, or finally, to give a formal command?

The faithful may be surprised at first by these shades of meaning. On reflection they will understand the subtlety and discretion with which the authority of the living magisterium is used and the respect it shows for the freedom of the children of God whom it has the mission to guide in a spirit of love.

But how are these degrees of authority to be recognized in the document itself?

Very often the expressions used by the popes are themselves sufficient to make known his intention and will. Father Villain, in the book already mentioned, uses as an example the Letter of the Congregation of Council (1929) to Cardinal Lienart, which contains these different nuances; "The Church holds it morally necessary ... The Church exhorts ... the Church wishes ... the Church suggests ... the Church recommends."

Then a clear distinction must be made between the different parts of the document; the doctrinal part and the technical or economic part. The pope does not invoke his authority in those exposès, generally very brief, of a technical or economic nature which are delivered just to frame the question. But whatever touches doctrine, on the contrary, belongs to the ordinary magisterium.

Finally, the nature of the intervention of the pope and the form chosen by him must be considered, whether it be an Encyclical, an allocution or a letter.

Of course the most solemn form is the Encyclical. For the Church's social teaching we know the great Encyclicals of Leo XIII (*Rerum Novarum*), Pius X (The Social Question), Pius XI (*Quadragesimo Anno—Divini Redemptoris*)

John XXIII (*Mater et Magistra*). Pius XII did not write a specific Encyclical on the social question but several of his Encyclicals, beginning with *Summi Pontificatus*, contain important passages on social problems.

Furthermore, Pius XII often preferred the form of radio messages for his great teachings in order, as he explained it himself, to overcome by the spoken word the barriers raised by war, hot or cold, as regards written documents.

Now, contrary to what many think, a radio message may have as much authority as an Encyclical. Just think of the doctrinal riches of the great Christmas radio messages. With regard to them the duty of Christians is the same.

As for allocutions, it can be said that they are of two kinds.

In some the pope particularly wants to affirm the Church's presence in contemporary life, his benevolent and paternal attention to different walks of life, his care as Pastor for their problems, their difficulties and their place in national life—these are the *pastoral* allocutions: (e.g. to pilgrimages and to certain professions). As against this, in other allocutions the pope wants to give a true teaching on a doctrinal problem, not only to those present, but to all the faithful. These are the *doctrinal* allocutions: e.g. the discourses to doctors where Pius XII dealt with artificial insemination, therapeutic abortion, painless child-birth, anaesthesia, psychoanalysis etc., in short, a whole "deontology" was taught. On the plane of social teaching there are the discourses to different professions (employers, technicians, craftsmen, workers, farmers, businessmen etc....) or to Congresses (Financial, International Exchanges, Humanistic Studies, Administrative Sciences, International Law, etc.) or Letters to Social Study Weeks.

All the documents which we have quoted fall into this category of *doctrinal* discourses, allocutions and letters.

3) When any document, no matter what its form (encyclical, radio message, allocution or letter) is doctrinal in character, whenever the desire of the Holy Father to invoke his authority in pronouncing on some point of doctrine is obvious and wherever we find a true continuity in the teaching of successive popes, as in the case of the Church's social teaching, such an act of the ordinary magisterium calls for acceptance and practical obedience on the part of the faithful. A respectful silence in not enough. Here again perhaps the living magisterium can itself distinguish the degrees and shades in the expression of its intervention. But the faithful Catholic who tries to conform dutifully to the intention and will of the head of the Church will receive this teaching in filial spirit, assimilate and practise it, taking the pope's warning and counsels into account. He will derive enlightenment, strength and courage to remain *himself* in the midst of the forces ranged against faith in the struggle of life. He will understand and often even discover for the first time his noble mission in the construction of a more human society.

In the present confusion of minds and dangers which threaten the world, the Catholic will be proud to manifest the light of the social teaching of the Church and to benefit from her maternal care, anxious as she is to guide her children in the social, economic and political order which also affects the salvation of all mankind.

"Mater et Magistra"

ENCYCLICAL LETTER OF POPE JOHN XXIII

On Recent Developments of the Social Question
in the Light of Christian Teaching

*To Our Venerable Brothers, the Patriarchs, Primates
Archbishops, Bishops and Other Local Ordinaries
in Peace and Communion with the Holy See,
and to All the Clergy and Faithful of the Catholic World:*

POPE JOHN XXIII

*Venerable Brothers and Dear Sons:
Health and Apostolic Benediction*

THE CATHOLIC CHURCH has been established by Jesus Christ as
MOTHER AND TEACHER of nations, so that all who in the course
of centuries come to her loving embrace, may find salvation as
well as the fullness of a more excellent life. To this Church, "the
pillar and mainstay of the truth," [1] her most holy Founder has
entrusted the double task of begetting sons unto herself, and of
educating and governing those whom she begets, guiding with
maternal providence the life both of individuals and of peoples.
The lofty dignity of this life, she has always held in the highest
respect and guarded with watchful care.

2. For the teaching of Christ joins, as it were, earth with
heaven, in that it embraces the whole man, namely, his soul and
body, intellect and will, and bids him to lift up his mind from
the changing conditions of human existence to that heavenly
country where he will one day enjoy unending happiness and
peace.

3. Hence, although Holy Church has the special task of sanctifying souls and of making them sharers of heavenly blessings, she

---

1 Cf. 1 Tim. 3, 15.

is also solicitous for the requirements of men in their daily lives, not merely those relating to food and sustenance, but also to their comfort and advancement in various kinds of goods and in varying circumstances of time.

4. Realizing all this, Holy Church implements the commands of her Founder, Christ who refers primarily to man's eternal salvation when He says, "I am the Way, and the Truth, and the Life" [2] and elsewhere "I am the Light of the World." [3] On other occasions, however, seeing the hungry crowd, He was moved to exclaim sorrowfully, "I have compassion on the crowd," [4] thereby indicating that He was also concerned about the earthly needs of mankind. The divine Redeemer shows this care not only by His words but also by the actions of His life, as when, to alleviate the hunger of the crowds, He more than once miraculously multiplied bread.

5. By this bread, given for the nourishment of the body, He wished to foreshadow that heavenly food of the soul which He was to give to men on *the day before He suffered.*

6. It is no wonder, then, that the Catholic Church, instructed by Christ and fulfilling His commands, has for two thousand years, from the ministry of the early deacons to the present time, tenaciously held aloft the torch of charity not only by her teaching but also by her widespread example—that charity which, by combining in a fitting manner the precepts and the practice of mutual love, puts into effect in a wonderful way this twofold commandment of *giving,* wherein is contained the full social teaching and action of the Church.

7. By far the most notable evidence of this social teaching and action, which the Church has set forth through the centuries,

---

2 John 14, 6.
3 John 8, 12.
4 Mark 8, 2.

undoubtedly is the very distinguished Encyclical Letter *Rerum Novarum,* [5] issued seventy years ago by our predecessor of immortal memory, Leo XIII. Therein he put forward teachings whereby the question of the workers' condition would be resolved in conformity with Christian principles.

8. Seldom have the admonitions of a Pontiff been received with such universal approbation, as was that Encyclical of Leo XIII, rivaled by few in the depth and scope of its reasoning and in the forcefulness of its expression. Indeed, the norms and recommendations contained therein were so momentous that their memory will never fall into oblivion. As a result, the action of the Catholic Church became more widely known. For its Supreme Pastor, making his own the problems of weak and harassed men, their complaints and aspirations, had devoted himself especially to the defense and restoration of their rights.

9. Even today, in spite of the long lapse of time since the Letter was published, much of its effectiveness is still evident. It is indeed evident in the documents of the popes who succeeded Leo XIII, and who, when they discussed economic and social affairs, have always borrowed something from it, either to clarify its application or to stimulate further activity on the part of Catholics. The efficacy of the document also is evident in the laws and institutions of many nations. Thus does it become abundantly clear that the solidly grounded principles, the norms of action, and the paternal admonitions found in the masterly Letter of our predecessor, even today retain their original worth. Moreover, from it can be drawn new and vital criteria, whereby men may judge the nature and extent of the social question, and determine what their responsibilities are in this regard.

---

5 Acta Leonis XIII, XI (1891), p. 97-144.

PART I

TEACHINGS OF THE ENCYCLICAL
"RERUM NOVARUM"
AND TIMELY DOCTRINAL DEVELOPMENTS
DURING THE PONTIFICATES OF
PIUS XI AND PIUS XII

THE PERIOD OF THE ENCYCLICAL, "RERUM NOVARUM"

10. The teachings addressed to mankind by this most wise Pontiff undoubtedly shone with greater brilliance because they were published when innumerable difficulties obscured the issue. On the one hand, the economic and political situation was in process of radical change; on the other, numerous clashes were flaring up and civil strife had been provoked.

11. As is generally known, in those days an opinion widely prevailed and was commonly put into practice, according to which, in economic matters, everything was to be attributed to inescapable, natural forces. Hence, it was held that no connection existed between economic and moral laws. Wherefore, those engaged in economic activity need look no further than their own gain. Consequently, mutual relations between economic agents could be left to the play of free and unregulated competition. Interest on capital, prices of goods and services, profits and wages, were to be determined purely mechanically by the laws of the marketplace. Every precaution was to be taken lest the civil authority intervene in any way in economic affairs. During that era, trade unions, according to circumstances in

different countries, were sometimes forbidden, sometimes tolerated, sometimes recognized in private law.

12. Thus, at that time, not only was the proud rule of the stronger regarded as legitimate, so far as economic affairs were concerned, but it also prevailed in concrete relations between men. Accordingly, the order of economic affairs was, in general, radically disturbed.

13. While a few accumulated excessive riches, large masses of workingmen daily labored in very acute need. Indeed, wages were insufficient for the necessities of life, and sometimes were at starvation level. For the most part, workers had to find employment under conditions wherein there were dangers to health, moral integrity, and religious faith. Especially inhuman were the working conditions to which children and women were subjected. The spectre of unemployment was ever present, and the family was exposed to a process of disorganization.

14. As a natural consequence, workers indignant at their lot, decided that this state of affairs must be publicly protested. This explains why, among the working classes, extremist theories that propounded remedies worse than the evil to be cured, found widespread favor.

The Way to Reconstruction

15. Such being the trend of the times, Leo XIII, in his Encyclical Letter *Rerum Novarum*, proclaimed a social message based on the requirements of human nature itself and conforming to the precepts of the Gospel and reason. We recall it as a message which, despite some expected opposition, evoked response on all sides and aroused widespread enthusiasm. However, this was not the first time the Apostolic See, in regard to the affairs of this life, undertook the defense of the needy, since

that same predecessor of happy memory, Leo XIII, published other documents which to some extent paved the way for the document mentioned above. But this Letter so effected for the first time an organization of principles, and, as it were, set forth singlemindedly a future course of action, that we may regard it as a summary of Catholic teaching, so far as economic and social matters are concerned.

16. It can be said with considerable assurance that such proved to be the situation. For while some, confronted with the social question, unashamedly attacked the Church as if she did nothing except preach resignation to the poor and exhort the rich to generosity, Leo XIII did not hesitate to proclaim and defend quite openly the sacred rights of workers. In beginning his exposition of the principles and norms of the Church in social matters. ho frankly stated: "We approach the subject with confidence and in the exercise of the rights that belong to us. For no satisfactory solution of this question will ever be found without the assistance of religion and the Church." [6]

17. Venerable Brothers, you are quite familiar with those basic principles expounded both clearly and auhoritatively by the illustrious Pontiff, according to which human society should be renewed in so far as economic and social matters are concerned.

18. He first and foremost stated that work, inasmuch as it is an expression of the human person, can by no means be regarded as a mere commodity. For the great majority of mankind, work is the only source from which the means of livelihood are drawn. Hence, its remuneration is not to be thought of in terms of merchandise, but rather according to the laws of justice and equity. Unless this is done, justice is violated in labor agreements, even though they are entered into freely on both sides.

---

[6] *Ibid.*, p. 107.

19. Private property, including that of productive goods, is a natural right possessed by all, which the State may by no means suppress. However, as there is from nature a social aspect to private property, he who uses his right in this regard must take into account not merely his own welfare but that of others as well.

20. The State, whose purpose is the realization of the common good in the temporal order, can by no means disregard the economic activity of its citizens. Indeed, it should be present to promote in suitable manner the production of a sufficient supply of material goods, "the use of which is necessary for the practice of virtue." [7] Moreover, it should safeguard the rights of all citizens, but especially the weaker, such as workers, women, and children. Nor may the State ever neglect its duty to contribute actively to the betterment of the living conditions of workers.

21. In addition, the State should see to it that labor agreements are entered into according to the norms of justice and equity, and that in the environment of work the dignity of the human being is not violated either in body or spirit. On this point, Leo XIII's Letter delineated the broad principles regarding a just and proper human existence. These principles, modern States have adopted in one way or another in their social legislation, and they have—as our predecessor of immortal memory, Pius XI declared, in his Encyclical Letter, *Quadragesimo Anno* [8]—contributed much to the establishment and promotion of that new section of legal science known as *labor law*.

22. In the same Letter, moreover, there is affirmed the natural right to enter corporately into associations, whether these be composed of workers only or of workers and management: and also the right to adopt that organizational structure judged more suitable to meet their professional needs. And workers themselves

---

7 St. Thomas, *De regimine principum*, I, 15.
8 Cf. *Acta Apostolicae Sedis*, XXIII (1931), p. 185.

have the right to act freely and on their own initiative within the above-mentioned associations, without hindrance and as their needs dictate.

23. Workers and employers should regulate their mutual relations in a spirit of human solidarity and in accordance with the bond of Christian brotherhood. For the unregulated competition which so-called *liberals* espouse, or the class struggle in the *Marxist sense,* are utterly opposed to Christian teaching and also to the very nature of man.

24. These, Venerable Brothers, are the fundamental principles on which a healthy socio-economic order can be built.

25. It is not surprising, therefore, that outstanding Catholic men inspired by these appeals began many activities in order to put these principles to action. Nor were there lacking other men of good will in various parts of the world who, impelled by the needs of human nature, followed a similar course.

26. For these reasons the Encyclical is known even to the present day as the *Magna Charta* [9] for the reconstruction of the economic and social order.

THE ENCYCLICAL "QUADRAGESIMO ANNO"

27. Furthermore, after a lapse of forty years since publication of that outstanding corpus, as it were, of directives, our predecessor of happy memory, Pius XI, in his turn decided to publish the Encyclical Letter *Quadragesimo Anno.* [10]

28. In it the Supreme Pontiff first of all confirmed the right and duty of the Catholic Church to make special contribution in resolving the more serious problems of society which call for the

---

9 Cf. *Ibid.,* p. 189.
10 *Ibid.,* p. 177-228.

full cooperation of all. Then he reaffirmed those principles and directives of Leo XIII's Letter related to the conditions of the times. Finally, he took this occasion not only to clarify certain points of doctrine on which even Catholics were in doubt, but he also showed how the principles and directives themselves regarding social affairs should he adapted to the changing times.

29. For, at that time, some were in doubt as to what should be the judgment of Catholics regarding private property, the wage system, and more especially, a type of moderate socialism.

30. Concerning private property, our predecessor reaffirmed its natural-law character. Furthermore, he set forth clearly and emphasized the social character and function of private ownership.

31. Turning to the wage system, after having rejected the view that would declare it unjust by its very nature, the Pontiff criticized the inhuman and unjust forms under which it was sometimes found. Moreover, he carefully indicated what norms and conditions were to be observed, lest the wage system stray from justice and equity.

32. In this connection, it is today advisable as our predecessor clearly pointed out, that work agreements be tempered in certain respects with partnership arrangements, so that "workers and officials become participants in ownership, or management, or share in some manner in profits." [11]

33. Of great theoretical and practical importance is the affirmation of Pius XI that "if the social and individual character of labor be overlooked, the efficiency of men can neither be justly appraised nor equitably recompensed." [12] Accordingly, in determining wages, justice definitely requires that, in addition to the

---

11 Cf. *Ibid.*, p. 199.
12 Cf. *Ibid.*, p. 200.

needs of the individual worker and his family, regard be had on the one hand for conditions within the productive enterprises wherein the workers labor; on the other hand, for the "public economic good" [13] in general.

34. Furthermore, the Supreme Bishop emphasized that the views of *communists,* as they are called, and of Christians are radically opposed. Nor may Catholics, in any way, give approbation to the teachings of *socialists* who seemingly profess more moderate views. From their basic outlook it follows that, inasmuch as the order of social life is confined to time, it is directed solely to temporal welfare; that since the social relationships of men pertain merely to the production of goods, human liberty is excessively restricted and the true concept of social authority is overlooked.

35. Pius XI was not unaware that, in the forty years that had elapsed since the appearance of Leo XIII's Letter, historical conditions had profoundly altered. In fact, unrestricted competition, because of its own inherent tendencies, had ended by almost destroying itself. It had caused a great accumulation of wealth and a corresponding concentration of power in the hands of a few who "are frequently not the owners, but only the trustees and directors of invested funds, who administer them at their good pleasure." [14]

36. Therefore, as the Supreme Pontiff noted, "economic power has been substituted for the free marketplace. Unbridled ambition for domination has replaced desire for gain; the whole economy has become harsh, cruel, and relentless in frightful measure." [15] Thus it happened that even public authorities were serving the interests of more wealthy men and that concentrations of wealth, to some extent, achieved power over all peoples.

---

13 Cf. *Ibid.,* p. 201.
14 Cf. *Ibid.,* p. 210f.
15 Cf. *Ibid.,* p. 211.

37. In opposition to this trend, the Supreme Pontiff laid down the following fundamental principles: the organization of economic affairs must be conformable to practical morality; the interests of individuals or of societies especially must be harmonized with the requirements of the common good. This evidently requires, as the teaching of our predecessor indicated, the orderly reorganization of society with smaller professional and economic groups existing in their own right, and not prescribed by public authority. In the next place, civil authority should reassume its function and not overlook any of the community's interests. Finally, on a world-wide scale, governments should seek the economic good of all peoples.

38. The two fundamental points that especially characterize the Encyclical of Pius XI are these: First, one may not take as the ultimate criteria in economic life the interests of individuals or organized groups, nor unregulated competition, nor excessive power on the part of the wealthy, nor the vain honor of the nation or its desire for domination, nor anything of this sort.

39. Rather, it is necessary that economic undertakings be governed by justice and charity as the principal laws of social life.

40. The second point that we consider to be basic to the Letter of Pius XI is that both within individual countries and among nations there be established a juridical order, with appropriate public and private institutions, inspired by social justice, so that those who are involved in economic activities are enabled to carry out their tasks in conformity with the common good.

RADIO BROADCAST OF PENTECOST, 1941

41. In specifying social rights and obligations, our predecessor of immortal memory, Pius XII, made a significant contribution, when on the feast of Pentecost, June 1, 1941, he broadcast

to the world community a message: "in order to call to the attention of the Catholic world the memory of an event worthy of being written in letters of gold on the Calendar of the Church: namely, the fiftieth anniversary of the publication of the epoch-making Encyclical of Leo XIII, *Rerum Novarum*." [16] He broadcast this message, moreover, "to render special thanks to Almighty God that His Vicar on earth, in a Letter such as this, gave to the Church so great a gift, and also to render praise to the eternal Spirit that through this same Letter, He enkindled a fire calculated to rouse the whole human race to new and better effort." [17]

42. In the message, the great Pontiff claimed for the Church "the indisputable competence" to "decide whether the bases of a given social system are in accord with the unchangeable order which God our Creator and Redeemer has fixed both in the natural law and revelation." [18] He noted that the Letter of Leo XIII is of permanent value and has rich and abiding usefulness. He takes the occasion "to explain in greater detail what the Catholic Church teaches regarding the three principal issues of social life in economic affairs, which are mutually related and connected one with the other, and thus interdependent: namely, the use of material goods, labor, and the family." [19]

43. Concerning the use of material goods, our predecessor declared that the right of every man to use them for his own sustenance is prior to all other rights in economic life, and hence is prior even to the right of private ownership. It is certain, however, as our predecessor noted, that the right of private property is from the natural law itself. Nevertheless, it is the will of God the Creator that this right to own property should in no wise

16 Cf. *Acta Apostolicae Sedis*, XXXIII (1941), p. 196.
17 Cf. *Ibid.*, p. 197.
18 Cf. *Ibid.*, p. 196.
19 Cf. *Ibid.*, p. 198f.

obstruct the flow of "material goods created by God to meet the needs of all men, to all equitably, as justice and charity require." [20]

44. As regards labor, Pius XII repeating what appeared in Leo XIII's Letter, declared it to be both a duty and a right of every human being. Consequently, it is in the first place the responsibility of men themselves to regulate mutual labor relations. Only in the event that the interested parties are unwilling or unable to fulfill their functions, does it "devolve upon the state to intervene and to assign labor equitably, safeguarding the standards and aims that the common good properly understood demands." [21]

45. Turning to the family, the Supreme Pontiff stresses that private ownership of material goods helps to safeguard and develop family life. Such goods are an apt means "to secure for the father of a family the healthy liberty he needs in order to fulfill the duties assigned him by the Creator, regarding the physical, spiritual, and religious welfare of the family." [22] From this arises the right of the family to migrate. Accordingly, our predecessor reminds governments, both those permitting emigration and those accepting immigrants, that "they never permit anything whereby mutual and sincere understanding between States is diminished or destroyed." [23] If this be mutually accomplished, it will come to pass that benefits are equalized and diffused widely among peoples, as the supply of goods and the arts and crafts are increased and fostered.

FURTHER CHANGES

46. But just as contemporary circumstances seemed to Pius XII quite dissimilar from those of the earlier period, so they have

---

20 Cf. *Ibid.*, p. 199.
21 Cf. *Ibid.*, p. 201
22 Cf. *Ibid.*, p. 202.
23 Cf. *Ibid.*, p. 203

changed greatly over the past twenty years. This can be seen not only in the internal situation of each individual country, but also in the mutual relations of countries.

47. In the fields of science, technology, and economics, these developments are especially worthy of note: the discovery of atomic energy, employed first for military purposes and later increasingly for peaceful ends; the almost limitless possibilities opened up by chemistry in synthetic products; the growth of automation in the sectors of industry and services; the modernization of agriculture; the nearly complete conquest, especially through radio and television, of the distance separating peoples; the greatly increased speed of all manner of transportation; the initial conquests of outer space.

48. Turning to the social field, the following contemporary trends are evident: development of systems for social insurance; the introduction of social systems in some more affluent countries; greater awareness among workers, as members of unions, of the principal issues in economic and social life; a progressive improvement of basic education; wider diffusion among the citizenry of the conveniences of life; increased social mobility and a resulting decline in divisions among the classes: greater interest than heretofore in world affairs on the part of those with average education. Meanwhile, if one considers the social and economic advances made in a growing number of countries, he will quickly discern increasingly pronounced imbalances: first, between agriculture on the one hand and industry and the services on the other; between the more and the less developed regions within countries; and, finally, on a worldwide scale, between countries with differing economic resources and development.

49. Turning now to political affairs, it is evident that there, too, a number of innovations have occurred. Today, in many communities, citizens from almost all social strata participate

in public life. Public authorities intervene more and more in economic and social affairs. The peoples of Asia and Africa, having set aside colonial systems, now govern themselves according to their own laws and institutions. As the mutual relationships of peoples increase, they become daily more dependent one upon the other. Throughout the world, assemblies and councils have become more common, which, being supranational in character, take into account the interests of all peoples. Such bodies are concerned with economic life, or with social affairs, or with culture and education, or, finally, with the mutual relationships of peoples.

REASONS FOR THE NEW ENCYCLICAL

50. Now, reflecting on all these things, we feel it our duty to keep alive the torch lighted by our great predecessors and to exhort all to draw from their writings light and inspiration, if they wish to resolve the social question in ways more in accord with the needs of the present time. Therefore, we are issuing this present Letter not merely to commemorate appropriately the Encyclical Letter of Leo XIII, but also, in the light of changed conditions, both to confirm and explain more fully what our predecessors taught, and to set forth the Church's teaching regarding the new and serious problems of our day.

Part II

PRIVATE INITIATIVE AND STATE INTERVENTION IN ECONOMIC LIFE

51. At the outset it should be affirmed that in economic affairs first place is to be given to the private initiative of individual men who, either working by themselves, or with others in one fashion or another, pursue their common interests.

52. But in this matter, for reasons pointed out by our predecessors, it is necessary that public authorities take active interest, the better to increase output of goods and to further social progress for the benefit of all citizens.

53. This intervention of public authorities that encourages, stimulates, regulates, supplements, and complements, is based on the *principle of subsidiarity* [24] as set forth by Pius XI in his Encyclical *Quadragesimo Anno*: "It is a fundamental principle of social philosophy, fixed and unchangeable, that one should not withdraw from individuals and commit to the community what they can accomplish by their own enterprise and industry. So, too, it is an injustice and at the same time a grave evil and a disturbance of right order, to transfer to the larger and higher collectivity functions which can be performed and provided for by lesser and subordinate bodies. Inasmuch as every social activity should, by its very nature, prove a help to members of the body social, it should never destroy or absorb them." [25]

---

24 *Acta Apostolicae Sedis*, XXIII (1931), p. 203.
25 *Ibid.*, p. 203.

54. Indeed, as is easily perceived, recent developments of science and technology provide additional reasons why, to a greater extent than heretofore, it is within the power of public authorities to reduce imbalances, whether these be between various sectors of economic life, or between different regions of the same nation, or even between different peoples of the world as a whole. These same developments make it possible to keep fluctuations in the economy within bounds, and to provide effective measures for avoiding mass unemployment. Consequently, it is requested again and again of public authorities responsible for the common good, that they intervene in a wide variety of economic affairs, and that, in a more extensive and organized way than heretofore, they adapt institutions, tasks, means, and procedures to this end.

55. Nevertheless, it remains true that precautionary activities of public authorities in the economic field, although widespread and penetrating, should be such that they not only avoid restricting the freedom of private citizens, but also increase it, so long as the basic rights of each individual person are preserved inviolate. Included among these is the right and duty of each individual normally to provide the necessities of life for himself and his dependents. This implies that whatever be the economic system, it allow and facilitate for every individual the opportunity to engage in productive activity.

56. Furthermore, the course of events thus far makes it clear that there cannot be a prosperous and well-ordered society unless both private citizens and public authorities work together in economic affairs. Their activity should be characterized by mutual and amicable efforts, so that the roles assigned to each fit in with requirements of the common good, as changing times and customs suggest.

57. Experience, in fact, shows that where private initiative of individuals is lacking, political tyranny prevails. Moreover, much

stagnation occurs in various sectors of the economy, and hence all sorts of consumer goods and services, closely connected with needs of the body and more especially of the spirit, are in short supply. Beyond doubt, the attainment of such goods and services provides remarkable opportunity and stimulus for individuals to exercise intiative and industry.

58. Where, on the other hand, appropriate activity of the state is lacking or defective, commonwealths are apt to experience incurable disorders, and there occurs exploitation of the weak by the unscrupulous strong, who flourish, unfortunately, like cockle among the wheat, in all times and places.

COMPLEXITY OF SOCIAL STRUCTURE

Direction of the trend

59. One of the principal characteristics of our time is the multiplication of social relationships, that is, a daily more complex interdependence of citizens, introducing into their lives and activities many and varied forms of association, recognized for the most part in private and even in public law. This tendency seemingly stems from a number of factors operative in the present era, among which are technical and scientific progress, greater productive efficiency, and a higher standard of living among citizens.

60. These developments in social living are at once both a symptom and a cause of the growing intervention of public authorities in matters which, since they pertain to the more intimate aspects of personal life, are of serious moment and not without danger. Such, for example, are the care of health, the instruction and education of youth, the choice of a personal career, the ways and means of rehabilitating or assisting those handicapped mentally or physically. But this trend also indicates

and in part follows from that human and natural inclination, scarcely resistible, whereby men are impelled voluntarily to enter into association in order to attain objectives which each one desires, but which exceed the capacity of single individuals. This tendency has given rise, especially in recent years, to organizations and institutes on both national and international levels, which relate to economic and social goals, to cultural and recreational activities, to athletics, to various professions, and to political affairs.

Evaluation

61. Such an advance in social relationships definitely brings numerous services and advantages. It makes possible, in fact, the satisfaction of many personal rights, especially those of economic and social life; these relate, for example, to the minimum necessities of human life, to health services, to the broadening and deepening of elementary education, to a more fitting training in skills, to housing, to labor, to suitable leisure and recreation. In addition, through the ever more perfect organization of modern means for the diffusion of thought—press, cinema, radio, television—individuals are enabled to take part in human events on a world-wide scale.

62. But as these various forms of association are multiplied and daily extended, it also happens that in many areas of activity, rules and laws controlling and determining relationships of citizens are multiplied. As a consequence, opportunity for free action by individuals is restricted within narrower limits. Methods are often used, procedures are adopted, and such an atmosphere develops wherein it becomes difficult for one to make decisions independently of outside influences, to do anything on his own initiative, to carry out in a fitting way his rights and duties, and to fully develop and perfect his personality. Will men perhaps, then become automatons, and cease to be personally

responsible, as these social relationships multiply more and more? It is a question which must be answered negatively.

63. Actually, increased complexity of social life by no means results from a blind drive of natural forces. Indeed, as stated above, it is the creation of free men who are so disposed to act by nature as to be responsible for what they do. They must, of course, recognize the laws of human progress and the development of economic life and take these into account. Furthermore, men are not altogether free of their milieu.

64. Accordingly, advances in social organization can and should be so brought about that maximum advantages accrue to citizens while at the same time disadvantages are averted or at least minimized.

65. That these desired objectives be more readily obtained, it is necessary that public authorities have a correct understanding of the common good. This embraces the sum total of those conditions of social living, whereby men are enabled more fully and more readily to achieve their own perfection. Hence, we regard it as necessary that the various intermediary bodies and the numerous social undertakings wherein an expanded social structure primarily finds expression, be ruled by their own laws, and as the common good itself progresses, pursue this objective in a spirit of sincere concord among themselves. Nor is it less necessary that the above mentioned groups present the form and substance of a true community. This they will do, only if individual members are considered and treated as persons, and are encouraged to participate in the affairs of the group.

66. Accordingly, as relationships multiply between men, binding them more closely together, commonwealths will more readily and appropriately order their affairs to the extent these two factors are kept in balance: (1) the freedom of individual citizens and groups of citizens to act autonomously, while cooperating one

with the other; (2) the activity of the State whereby the undertakings of private individuals and groups are suitably regulated and fostered.

67. Now if social systems are organized in accordance with the above norms and moral laws, their extension does not necessarily mean that individual citizens will be gravely discriminated against or excessively burdened. Rather, we can hope that this will enable man not only to develop and perfect his natural talents, but also will lead to an appropriate structuring of the human community. Such a structure, as our predecessor of happy memory, Pius XI, warned in his Encyclical Letter *Quadragesimo Anno*, [26] is absolutely necessary for the adequate fulfillment of the rights and duties of social life.

REMUNERATION FOR WORK

Standards of Justice and Equity

68. Our heart is filled with profound sadness when we observe, as it were, with our own eyes a wretched spectacle indeed —great masses of workers who, in not a few nations, and even in whole continents, receive too small a return from their labor. Hence, they and their families must live in conditions completely out of accord with human dignity. This can be traced, for example to the fact that, in these regions, modern industrial techniques either have only recently been introduced or have made less than satisfactory progress.

69. It happens in some of these nations that, as compared with the extreme need of the majority, the wealth and conspicuous consumption of a few stand out, and are in open and bold contrast with the lot of the needy. It happens in other places that excessive burdens are placed upon men in order that the

---

26 Cf. *Ibid.*, p. 222f.

commonwealth may achieve, within a brief span, an increase of wealth such as can by no means be achieved without violating the laws of justice and equity. Finally, it happens elsewhere that a disproportionate share of the revenue goes toward the building up of national prestige, and that large sums of money are devoted to armaments.

70. Moreover, in the economically developed countries, it frequently happens that great, or sometimes very great, remuneration is had for the performance of some task of lesser importance or doubtful utility. Meanwhile, the diligent and profitable work that whole classes of decent and hard-working citizens perform, receives too low a payment and one insufficient for the necessities of life, or else, one that does not correspond to the contribution made to the community, or to the revenues of the undertakings in which they are engaged, or to the national income.

71. Wherefore, we judge it to be our duty to reaffirm once again that just as remuneration for work cannot be left entirely to unregulated competition, neither may it be decided arbitrarily at the will of the more powerful. Rather, in this matter, the norms of justice and equity should be strictly observed. This requires that workers receive a wage sufficient to lead a life worthy of man and to fulfill family responsibilities properly. But in determining what constitutes an appropriate wage, the following must necessarily be taken into account: first of all, the contribution of individuals to the economic effort; the economic state of the enterprises within which they work; the requirements of each community, especially as regards over-all employment; finally, what concerns the common good of all peoples, namely, of the various States associated among themselves, but differing in character and extent.

72. It is clear that the standards of judgment set forth above are binding always and everywhere. However, the measure in

which they are to be applied in concrete cases cannot be established unless account is taken of the resources at hand. These resources can and in fact do vary in quantity and quality among different peoples, and may even change within the same country with the passing of time.

Balancing Economic Developement and Social Progress

73. Whereas in our era the economies of various countries are evolving very rapidly, more especially since the last great war, we take this opportunity to draw the attention of all to a strict demand of social justice, which explicitly requires that, with the growth of the economy, there occur a corresponding social development. Thus, all classes of citizens will benefit equitably from an increase in national wealth. Toward this end vigilance should be exercised and effective steps taken that class differences arising from disparity of wealth not be increased, but lessened so far as possible.

74. "National wealth"—as our predecessor of happy memory, Pius XII, rightfully observed—"inasmuch as it is produced by the common efforts of the citizenry, has no other purpose than to secure without interruption those material conditions in which individuals are enabled to lead a full and perfect life. Where this is consistently the case, then such a people is to be judged truly rich. For the system whereby both the common prosperity is achieved and individuals exercise their right to use material goods, conforms fully to norms laid down by God the Creator." [27] From this it follows that the economic prosperity of any people is to be assessed not so much from the sum total of goods and wealth possessed as from the distribution of goods according to norms of justice, so that everyone in the community can develop and perfect himself. For this, after all, is the end toward which all economic activity of a community is by nature ordered.

---

27 Cf. *Acta Apostolicae Sedis*, XXXIII (1941), p. 200.

75. We must here call attention to the fact that in many countries today, the economic system is such that large and medium sized productive enterprises achieve rapid growth precisely because they finance replacement and plant expansion from their own revenues. Where this is the case, we believe that such companies should grant to workers some share in the enterprise, especially where they are paid no more than the minimum wage.

76. In this matter, the principle laid down by our predecessor of happy memory, Pius XI, in the Encyclical Letter *Quadragesimo Anno*, should be borne in mind: "It is totally false to ascribe to a single factor of production what is in fact produced by joint activity; and it is completely unjust for one factor to arrogate to itself what is produced, ignoring what has been contributed by other factors." [28]

77. The demands of justice referred to, can be met in various ways, as experience shows. Not to mention other ways, it is very desirable that workers gradually acquire some share in the enterprise by such methods as seem more appropriate. For today, more than in the times of our predecessor, "every effort should be made that at least in the future, only an equitable share of the fruits of production accumulate in the hands of the wealthy, and a sufficient and ample portion go to the workingmen." [29]

78. But we should remember that adjustments between remuneration for work and revenues are to be brought about in conformity with the requirements of the common good, both of one's own community and of the entire human family.

79. Considering the common good on the national level, the following points are relevant and should not be overlooked: to provide employment for as many workers as possible; to take

28 *Acta Apostolicae Sedis,* XXIII (1931), p. 195.
29 *Ibid.,* p. 198.

care lest privileged groups arise even among the workers themselves; to maintain a balance between wages and prices; to make accessible the goods and services for a better life to as many persons as possible; either to eliminate or to keep within bounds the inequalities that exist between different sectors of the economy—that is, between agriculture, industry and services; to balance properly any increases in output with advances in services provided to citizens, especially by public authority; to adjust, as far as possible, the means of production to the progress of science and technology; finally, to ensure that the advantages of a more humane way of existence not merely subserve the present generation but have regard for future generations as well.

80. As regards the common good of human society as a whole, the following conditions should be fulfilled: that the competitive striving of peoples to increase output be free of bad faith; that harmony in economic affairs and a friendly and beneficial cooperation be fostered; and, finally, that effective aid be given in developing the economically underdeveloped nations.

81. It is evident from what has been said that these demands of the common good, on both the national and world levels, should be borne in mind, when there is question of determining the share of earning assigned to those responsible for directing the productive enterprise, or as interest and dividends to those who have invested capital.

DEMANDS OF JUSTICE AS REGARDS
PRODUCTIVE INSTITUTIONS

Institutions Conforming to the Dignity of Man

82. Justice is to be observed not merely in the distribution of wealth, but also in regard to the conditions under which men engage in productive activity. There is, in fact, an innate need

of human nature requiring that men engaged in productive activity have an opportunity to assume responsibility and to perfect themselves by their efforts.

83. Consequently, if the human dignity of workers is compromised, or their sense of responsibility is weakened, or their freedom of action is removed, then we judge such an economic order to be unjust, even though it produces a vast amount of goods, whose distribution conforms to the norms of justice and equity.

Reaffirmation of a Directive

84. Nor is it possible in economic affairs to determine in one formula all the measures that are more conformable to the dignity of man, or are more suitable in developing in him a sense of responsibility. Nevertheless, our predecessor of happy memory, Pius XII, appropriately laid down certain norms of action: "Small and medium-sized holdings in agriculture, in the arts and crafts, in commerce and industry, should be safeguarded and fostered. Such enterprises should join together in mutual-aid societies in order that the services and benefits of large-scale enterprises will be available to them. So far as these larger enterprises are concerned, work agreements should in some way be modified by partnership arrangements." [30]

Artisan Enterprises and Cooperative Associations

85. Wherefore, conformably to requirements of the common good and the state of technology, artisan and farm enterprises of family type should be safeguarded and fostered, as should also cooperatives that aim to complement and perfect such enterprises.

86. We shall return shortly to the subject of farm enterprises. Here, we think it appropriate to say something about artisan enterprises and cooperative associations.

---

30 Radio Broadcast, September 1, 1944; cf. A.A.S., XXXVI., (1944), p. 254.

87. Above all, it must be emphasized that enterprises and bodies of this sort, in order that they may survive and flourish, should be continuously adapted—both in their productive structure and in their operating methods—to new conditions of the times. These new conditions constantly arise from advances in science and technology, or from changing consumer needs and preferences. It is especially appropriate that all this be done by the craftsmen themselves and by the associates in the cooperatives.

88. Hence, it is most fitting not only that both these groups be suitably formed in technical and in spiritual and intellectual matters, but also that they be joined together professionally. Nor is it less fitting that the State make special provision for them in regard to instruction, taxes, credit facilities, social security and insurance.

89. Moreover, the measures taken by the State on behalf of the craftsmen and members of cooperatives are also justified by the fact that these two categories of citizens are producers of genuine wealth, and contribute to the advance of civilization.

90. Accordingly, we paternally exhort our beloved sons, craftsmen and members of cooperatives throughout the world, that they fully realize the dignity of their role in society, since, by their work, the sense of responsibility and spirit of mutual aid can be daily more intensified among the citizenry, and the desire to work with dedication and originality be kept alive.

Participation of Workers in Medium-size and Large Enterprises

91. Furthermore, as did our predecessors, we regard as justifiable the desire of employees to be partners in enterprises with

which they are associated and wherein they work. We do not think it possible, however, to decide with certain and explicit norms the manner and degree of such partnership, since this must be determined according to the state of the individual productive enterprises. For the situation is not everywhere the same, and, in fact, it can change suddenly within one and the same enterprise. Nevertheless, we do not doubt that employees should have an active part in the affairs of the enterprise wherein they work, whether these be private or public. But it is of the utmost importance that productive enterprises assume the character of a true human fellowship whose spirit suffuses the dealings, activities, and standing of all its members.

92. This requires that mutual relations between employers and directors on the one hand and the employees of the enterprise on the other, be marked by mutual respect, esteem, and good will. It also demands that all collaborate sincerely and harmoniously in their joint undertaking, and that they perform their work not merely with the objective of deriving an income, but also of carrying out the role assigned them and of performing a service that results in benefit to others. This means that the workers may have a say in, and may make a contribution toward, the efficient running and development of the enterprise. Thus, our predecessor of happy memory, Pius XII, clearly indicated: "The economic and social functions which everyone aspires to fulfill, require that efforts of individuals be not wholly subjected to the will of others." [31] Beyond doubt, an enterprise truly in accord with human dignity should safeguard the necessary and efficient unity of administration. But it by no means follows that those who work daily in such an enterprise are to

---

[31] Allocution, October 8, 1956; cf. A.A.S. XLVIII (1956), p. 799-800.

be considered merely as servants, whose sole function is to execute orders silently, and who are not allowed to interject their desires and interests, but must conduct themselves as idle standbys when it comes to assignment and direction of their tasks.

93. Finally, attention is drawn to the fact that the greater amount of responsibility desired today by workers in productive enterprises, not merely accords with the nature of man, but also is in conformity with historical developments in the economic, social, and political fields.

94. Unfortunately, in our day, there occur in economic and social affairs many imbalances that militate against justice and humanity. Meanwhile, throughout all of economic life, errors are spread that seriously impair its operation, purposes, organization, and the fulfillment of responsibilities. Nevertheless, it is an undeniable fact that the more recent productive systems, thanks to the impulse deriving from advances in technology and science, are becoming more modern and efficient, and are expanding at a faster rate than in the past. This demands of workers greater abilities and professional qualifications. Accordingly, workers should be provided with additional aids and time to achieve a suitable and more rounded formation, and to carry out more fittingly their duties as regards studies, morals, and religion.

95. Thus it happens that in our day youths can be allotted additional years to acquire a basic education and necessary skills.

96. Now if these things be done, a situation will emerge wherein workers are enabled to assume greater responsibilities even within their own enterprises. As regards the commonwealth as such, it is of great importance that all ranks of citizens feel themselves daily more obligated to safeguard the common good.

Participation of Workers at All Levels

97. Now, as is evident to all, in our day association of workers have become widespread, and for the most part have been given

legal status within individual countries and even across national boundaries. These bodies no longer recruit workers for purposes of strife, but rather for pursuing a common aim. And this is achieved especially by collective bargaining between associations of workers and those of management. But it should be emphasized how necessary, or at least very appropriate, it is to give workers an opportunity to exert influence outside the limits of the individual productive unit, and indeed within all ranks of the commonwealth.

98. The reason is that individual productive units, whatever their size, efficiency, or importance within the commonwealth, are closely connected with the over-all economic and social situation in each country, whereon their own prosperity ultimately depends.

99. Nevertheless, to decide what is more helpful to the over-all economic situation is not the prerogative of individual productive enterprises, but pertains to the public authorities and to those institutions which, established either nationally or among a number of countries, function in various sectors of economic life. From this is evident the propriety or necessity of ensuring that not only managers or agents of management are represented before such authorities and institutions, but also workers or those who have the responsibility of safeguarding the rights, needs, and aspirations of workers.

100. It is fitting, therefore, that our thoughts and paternal affection be directed toward the various professional groups and associations of workers which, in accord with principles of Christian teaching, carry on their activities on several continents. We are aware of the many and great difficulties experienced by these beloved sons of ours, as they effectively worked in the past and continue and strive, both within their national boundaries and throughout the world, to vindicate the rights of workingmen and to improve their lot and conduct.

101. Furthermore, we wish to give deserved praise to the work of these our sons. Their accomplishments are not always immediately evident, but nevertheless permeate practically the entire field of labor, spreading correct norms of action and thought, and the beneficial influence of the Christian religion.

102. And we wish also to praise paternally those dear sons of ours who, imbued with Christian principles, give their special attention to other labor associations and those groups of workingmen that follow the laws of nature and respect the religious and moral liberty of individuals.

103. Nor can we at this point neglect to congratulate and to express our esteem for the International Labor Organization— variously signified popularly by the letters O.I.L. or I.L.O. or O.I.T.—which, for many years, has done effective and valuable work in adapting the economic and social order everywhere to the norms of justice and humanity. In such an order, the legitimate rights of workers are recognized and preserved.

PRIVATE PROPERTY

Changed Conditions

104. In recent years, as we are well aware, the role played by the owners of capital in very large productive enterprises has been separated more and more from the role of management. This has occasioned great difficulties for governments, whose duty it is to make certain that directors of the principal enterprises, especially those of greatest influence in the economic life of the entire country, do not depart from the requirements of the common good. These difficulties, as we know from experience, are by no means less, whether it be private citizens or public bodies that make the capital investments requisite for large-scale enterprises.

105. It is also quite clear that today the number of persons is increasing who, because of recent advances in insurance programs and various systems of social security, are able to look to the future with tranquillity. This sort of tranquillity once was rooted in the ownership of property, albeit modest.

106. It sometimes happens in our day that men are more inclined to seek some professional skill than possession of goods. Moreover, such men have greater esteem for income from labor or rights arising from labor, than for that deriving from capital investment or rights associated therewith.

107. This clearly accords with the inherent characteristics of labor, inasmuch as this proceeds directly from the human person, and hence is to be thought more of than wealth in external goods. These latter, by their very nature, must be regarded as instruments. This trend indicates an advance in civilization.

108. Economic conditions of this kind have occasioned popular doubt as to whether, under present circumstances, a principle of economic and social life, firmly enunciated and defended by our predecessors, has lost its force or is to be regarded as of lesser moment; namely, the principle whereby it is established that men have from nature a right of privately owning goods, including those of a productive kind.

Confirmation of the Right of Private Property

109. Such a doubt has no foundation. For the right of private property, including that pertaining to goods devoted to productive enterprises, is permanently valid. Indeed, it is rooted in the very nature of things, whereby we learn that individual men are prior to civil society, and hence, that civil society is to be directed toward man as its end. Indeed, the right of private individuals to act freely in economic affairs is recognized in vain, unless they are at the same time given an opportunity of freely selecting and using things necessary for the exercise of this right.

Moreover, experience and history testify that where political regimes do not allow to private individuals the possession also of productive goods, the exercise of human liberty is violated or completely destroyed in matters of primary importance. Thus it becomes clear that in the right of property, the exercise of liberty finds both a safeguard and a stimulus.

110. This explains the fact that socio-political groups and associations which endeavor to reconcile freedom with justice within society, and which until recently did not uphold the right of private property in productive goods, have now, enlightened by the course of social events, modified their views and are disposed actually to approve this right.

111. Accordingly, we make our own the insistence of our predecessor of happy memory, Pius XII: "In defending the right of private property, the Church has in mind a very important ethical aim in social matters. She does not, of course, strive to uphold the present state of affairs as if it were an expression of the divine will. And even less does she accept the patronage of the affluent and wealthy, while neglecting the rights of the poor and needy.... The Church rather does intend that the institution of private property be such as is required by the plan of divine wisdom and the law of nature." [32] Private ownership should safeguard the rights of the human person, and at the same time make its necessary contribution to the establishment of right order in society.

112. While recent developments in economic life progress rapidly in a number of countries, as we have noted, and produce goods ever more efficiently, justice and equity require that remuneration for work also be increased within limits allowed by the common good. This enables workers to save more readily and

---

[32] Radio Broadcast, September 1, 1944; cf. A.A.S., XXXVI (1944), p. 253.

hence to achieve some property status of their own. Wherefore, it is indeed surprising that some reject the natural role of private ownership. For it is a right which continually draws its force and vigor from the fruitfulness of labor, and which, accordingly, is an effective aid in safeguarding the dignity of the human person and the free exercise of responsibility in all fields of endeavor. Finally, it strengthens the stability and tranquillity of family life, thus contributing to the peace and prosperity of the commonwealth.

Effective Distribution

113. It is not enough, then, to assert that man has from nature the right of privately possessing goods as his own, including those of productive character, unless, at the same time, a continuing effort is made to spread the use of this right through all ranks of the citizenry.

114. Our predecessor of happy memory, Pius XII, clearly reminded us that on the one hand the dignity of the human person necessarily "requires the right of using external goods in order to live according to the right norm of nature. And to this right corresponds a most serious obligation, which requires that, so far as possible, there be given to all an opportunity of possessing private property." [33] On the other hand, the nobility inherent in work, besides other requirements, demands "the conservation and perfection of a social order that makes possible a secure, although modest, property to all classes of the people." [34]

115. It is especially appropriate that today, more than heretofore, widespread private ownership should prevail, since, as noted above, the number of nations increases wherein the economic systems experience daily growth. Therefore, by prudent use of various devices already proven effective, it will not be

---

[33] Radio Broadcast, December 24, 1942; cf. A.A.S., XXXV (1943), p. 17.
[34] Cf. Ibid., p. 20.

difficult for the body politic to modify economic and social life so that the way is made easier for widespread private possession of such things as durable goods, homes gardens, tools requisite for artisan enterprises and family-type farms, investments in enterprises of medium or large size. All of this has occurred satisfactorily in some nations with developed social and economic systems.

Public Property

116. Obviously, what we have said above does not preclude ownership of goods pertaining to production of wealth by States and public agencies, especially "if these carry with them power too great to be left in private hands, without injury to the community at large." [35]

117. It seems characteristic of our times to vest more and more ownership of goods in the State and in other public bodies. This is partially explained by the fact that the common good requires public authorities to exercise ever greater responsiblities. However, in this matter, the *principle of subsidiarity*, already mentioned above, is to be strictly observed. For it is lawful for States and public corporations to expand their domain of ownership only when manifest and genuine requirements of the common good so require, and then with safeguards, lest the possession of private citizens be diminished beyond measure, or what is worse, destroyed.

118. Finally, we cannot pass over in silence the fact that economic enterprises undertaken by the State or by public corporations should be entrusted to citizens outstanding in skill and integrity, who will carry out their responsibilities to the commonwealth with a deep sense of devotion. Moreover, the activity of these men should be subjected to careful and continu-

---

35 Encyclical Letter *Quadragesimo Anno;* A.A.S., XXIII (1931), p. 214.

ing supervision, lest, in the administration of the State itself, there develop an economic imperialism in the hands of a few. For such a development is in conflict with the highest good of the commonwealth.

Social Function of Property

119. Our predecessors have always taught that in the right of private property there is rooted a social responsibility. Indeed, in the wisdom of God the Creator, the over-all supply of goods is assigned, first of all, that all men may lead a decent life. As our predecessor of happy memory, Leo XIII, clearly reminded us in the Encyclical Letter *Rerum Novarum*, "This is the heart of the matter: whoever has received from the divine bounty a larger share of blessings, whether these be corporal or external or gifts of the mind, has received them to use for his own perfection, and, at the same time, as the minister of God's providence, for the benefit of others. 'He who has a talent' (says St. Gregory the Great), 'let him take care that he hides it not; he who has abundance, let him arouse himself to mercy and generosity; he who has skill in managing affairs, let him make special effort to share the use and utility thereof with his neighbor.' " [36]

120. Although in our day, the role assigned the State and public bodies has increased more and and more, it by no means follows that the social function of private ownership is obsolescent, as some seem to think. For social responsibility in this matter derives its force from the very right of private property. Furthermore, it is quite clear that there always will be a wide range of difficult situations, as well as hidden and grave needs, which the manifold providence of the State leaves untouched, and of which it can in no way take account. Wherefore, there is always wide scope for humane action by private citizens and for Christian charity. Finally, it is evident that in stimulating efforts

---

[36] *Acta Leonis* XIII, XI (1891), p. 114.

relating to spiritual welfare, the work done by individual men or by private civic groups has more value than what is done by public authorities.

121. Moreover, it is well to recall here that the right of private ownership is clearly evident in the Gospels, which reveal Jesus Christ ordering the rich to share their goods with the poor so as to turn them into spiritual possessions: "Do not lay up for yourselves treasures on earth, where rust and moth consume, and where thieves break in and steal; but lay up for yourselves treasures in heaven, where neither rust nor moth consumes nor thieves break in and steal." [37] And the divine Master states that whatever is done for the poor is done for Him: "Amen I say to you, as long as you did it for one of these, the least of My brethren, you did it for Me." [38]

---

37 Matt. 6, 19-20.
38 Matt. 25,40.

PART III

NEW ASPECTS OF THE SOCIAL QUESTION

122. The progress of events and of time have made it increasingly evident that the relationships between workers and management in productive enterprises must be readjusted according to norms of justice and charity. But the same is also true of the systems whereby various types of economic activity and the differently endowed regions within a country ought to be linked together. Meanwhile, within the over-all human community, many nations with varied endowments have not made identical progress in their economic and social affairs.

JUST REQUIREMENTS IN THE MATTER OF INTERRELATED PRODUCTIVE SECTORS

Agriculture: A Depressed Sector

123. First of all, to lay down some norms in regard to agriculture, we would note that the over-all number of rural dwellers seemingly has not diminished. Beyond doubt, however many farmers have abandoned their rural birthplace, and seek out either the more populous centers or the cities themselves. Now since this is the case in almost all countries, and since it affects large numbers of human beings, problems concerning life and dignity of citizens arise, which are indeed difficult to overcome.

124. Thus, as economic life progresses and expands, the percentage of rural dwellers diminishes, while the great number of industrial and service workers increases. Yet, we feel that those

who transfer from rural activities to other productive enterprises often are motivated by reasons arising from the very evolution of economic affairs. Very often, however, they are caught up by various enticements of which the following are noteworthy: a desire to escape from a confined environment offering no prospect of a more comfortable life; the wish, so common in our age, to undertake new activities and to acquire new experiences; the attraction of quickly acquired goods and fortunes; a longing after a freer life, with the advantages that larger towns and cities usually provide. But there is no doubt about this point: rural dwellers leave the fields because nearly everywhere they see their affairs in a state of depression, both as regards labor productivity and the level of living of farm populations.

125. Accordingly, in this grave matter, about which enquiries are made in nearly all countries, we should first of all ask what is to be done to prevent so great imbalances between agriculture, industry, and the services in the matter of productive efficiency? Likewise, what can be done to minimize differences between the rural standard of living and that of city dwellers whose money income is derived from industry or some service or other? Finally, how can it be brought about that those engaged in agricultural pursuits no longer regard themselves as inferior to others? Indeed, rural dwellers should be convinced not only that they can strengthen and develop their personalities by their toil, but also that they can look forward to the future vicissitudes with confidence.

126. Accordingly, we judge it opportune in this connection to lay down some norms of permanent validity; although, as is evident, these must be adapted as various circumstances of time and place permit, or suggest, or absolutely require.

Provision for Essential Public Services

127. First, it is necessary that everyone, and especially public authorities, strive to effect improvements in rural areas as re-

gards the principal services needed by all. Such are, for example: highway construction; transport services; marketing facilities; pure drinking water; housing; medical services; elementary, trade, and professional schools; things requisite for religion and for recreation; finally, furnishings and equipmemt needed in the modern farm home. Where these requirements for a dignified farm life are lacking to rural dwellers, economic and social progress does not occur at all, or else very slowly. Under such conditions, nothing can be done to keep men from deserting the fields, nor can anyone readily estimate their number.

Gradual and Orderly Development
of the Economic System

128. It is desirable, moreover, that economic development of commonwealths proceed in orderly fashion, meanwhile preserving appropriate balance between the various sectors of the economy. In particular, care must be had that within the agricultural sector innovations are introduced as regards productive technology, whether these relate to productive methods, or to cultivation of the fields, or the equipment for the rural enterprise, as far as the over-all economy allows or requires. And all this should be done as far as possible, in accordance with technical advances in industry and in the various services.

129. In this way, agriculture not only absorbs a larger share of industrial output, but also demands a higher quality of services. In its turn, agriculture offers to the industrial and service sectors of the economy, as well as to the community as a whole, those products which in kind and in quantity better meet consumer needs. Thus, agriculture contributes to stability of the purchasing power of money, a very positive factor for the orderly development of the entire economic system.

130. By proceeding in this manner, the following advantages, among others, arise: first of all, it is easier to know the origins

and destinations of rural dwellers displaced by modernization of agriculture. Thereupon, they can be instructed in skills needed for other types of work. Finally, economic aids and helps will not be lacking for their intellectual and cultural development, so that they can fit into new social groups.

Appropriate Economic Policy

131. To achieve orderly progress in various sectors of economic life, it is absolutely necessary that as regards agriculture, public authorities give heed and take action in the following matters: taxes and duties, credit, insurance, prices, the fostering of requisite skills, and, finally, improved equipment for rural enterprises.

Taxation

132. As regards taxation, assessment according to ability to pay is fundamental to a just and equitable system.

133. But in determining taxes for rural dwellers, the general welfare requires public authorities to bear in mind that income in a rural economy is both delayed and subject to greater risk. Moreover, there is difficulty in finding capital so as to increase returns.

Capital at Suitable Interest

134. Accordingly, those with money to invest are more inclined to invest it in enterprises other than in the rural economy. And for the same reason, rural dwellers cannot pay high rates of interest. Nor are they generally able to pay prevailing market rates for capital wherewith to carry on and expand their operations. Wherefore, the general welfare requires that public authorities not merely make special provision for agricultural financing, but also for establishment of banks that provide capital to farmers at reasonable rates of interest.

Social Insurance and Social Security

135. It also seems necessary to make provision for a twofold insurance, one covering agricultural output, the other covering farmers and their families. Because, as experience shows, the income of individual farmers is, on the average, less than that of workers in industry and the services, it does not seem to be fully in accord with the norms of social justice and equity to provide farmers with insurance or social security benefits that are inferior to those of other classes of citizens. For those insurance plans or provisions that are established generally should not differ markedly one from the other, whatever be the economic sector wherein the citizens work, or from which they derive their income.

136. Moreover, since social security and insurance can help appreciably in distributing national income among the citizens according to justice and equity, these systems can be regarded as means whereby imbalances among various classes of citizens are reduced.

Price Protection

137. Since agricultural products have special characteristics, it is fitting that their price be protected by methods worked out by economic experts. In this matter, although it is quite helpful that those whose interest are involved take steps to safeguard themselves, setting up, as it were, appropriate goals, public authorities cannot stand entirely aloof from the stabilization procedure.

138. Nor should this be overlooked, that, generally speaking, the price of rural products is more a recompense for farmers, labor than for capital investment.

139. Thus, our predecessor of happy memory, Pius XI, touching on the welfare of the human community, appropriately notes

in his Encyclical Letter *Quadragesimo Anno,* that "a reasonable relationship between different wages here enters into consideration." But he immediately adds, "Intimately connected with this is a reasonable relationship between the prices obtained for the products of the various economic groups: agrarian, industrial, and so forth." [39]

140. Inasmuch as agricultural products are destined especially to satisfy the basic needs of men, it is necessary that their price be such that all can afford to buy them. Nevertheless, there is manifest injustice in placing a whole group of citizens, namely, the farmers, in an inferior economic and social status, with less purchasing power than required for a decent livelihood. This, indeed, is clearly contrary to the common good of the country.

Strengthening Farm Income

141. In rural areas it is fitting that industries be fostered and common services be developed that are useful in preserving, processing, and finally, in transporting farms products. There is need, moreover, to establish councils and activities relating to various sectors of economic and professional affairs. By such means, suitable opportunity is given farm families to supplement their incomes, and that within the milieu wherein they live and work.

Appropriate Organization of Farming Enterprises

142. Finally, no one person can lay down a universal rule regarding the way in which rural affairs should be definitely organized, since in these matters there exists considerable variation within each country, and the difference is even greater when we consider the various regions of the world. However, those who hold man and the family in proper esteem, whether this be

---

39 Cf. *Acta Apostolicae Sedis,* XXIII (1931), p. 202.

based upon nature alone, or also upon Christian principles, surely look toward some form of agricultural enterprise, and particularly of the family type, which is modeled upon the community of men wherein mutual relationships of members and the organization of the enterprise itself are conformed to norms of justice and Christian teaching. And these men strive mightily that such organization of rural life be realized as far as circumstances permit.

143. The family farm will be firm and stable only when it yields money income sufficient for decent and humane family living. To bring this about, it is very necessary that farmers generally receive instruction, be kept informed of new developments, and be technically assisted by trained men. It is also necessary that farmers form among themselves mutual-aid societies; that they establish professional associations; that they function efficiently in public life, that is, in various administrative bodies and in political affairs.

Rural Workers: Participants in Improving Conditions

144. We are of the opinion that in rural affairs, the principal agents and protagonists of economic improvement, of cultural betterment, or of social advance, should be the men personally involved, namely, the farmers themselves. To them it should be quite evident that their work is most noble, because it is undertaken, as it were, in the majestic temple of creation; because it often concerns the life of plants and animals, a life inexhaustible in its expression, inflexible in its laws, rich in allusions to God, Creator and Provider. Moreover, labor in the fields not only produces various foodstuffs wherewith humankind is nourished, but also furnishes an increasing supply of raw materials for industry.

145. Furthermore, this is a work endowed with a dignity of its own, for it bears a manifold relationship to the mechanical arts, chemistry, and biology: these must be continually adapted to the requirements of emerging situations because scientific and technological advance is of great importance in rural life. Work of this kind, moreover, possesses a special nobility because it requires farmers to understand well the course of the seasons and to adapt themselves to the same; that they await patiently what the future will bring; that they appreciate the importance and seriousness of their duties; that they constantly remain alert and ready for new developments.

Solidarity and Cooperation

146. Nor may it be overlooked that in rural areas, as indeed in every productive sector, farmers should join together in fellowships, especially when the family itself works the farm. Indeed, it is proper for rural workers to have a sense of solidarity. They should strive jointly to set up mutual-aid societies and professional associations. All these are very necessary either to keep rural dwellers abreast of scientific and technical progress, or to protect the prices of goods produced by their labor. Besides, acting in this manner, farmers are put on the same footing as other classes of workers who, for the most part, join together in such fellowships. Finally, by acting thus, farmers will achieve an importance and influence in public affairs proportionate to their own role. For today it is unquestionably true that the solitary voice speaks, as they say, to the winds.

Recognizing Demands of the Common Good

147. But when rural dwellers, just as other classes of workers, wish to make their influence and importance felt, they should never disregard moral duties or civil law. Rather they should strive to bring their rights and interests into line with the rights and needs of other classes, and to refer the same to the common

good. In this connection, farmers who strive vigorously to improve the yield of their farm may rightly demand that their efforts be aided and complemented by public authorities, provided they themselves keep in mind the common needs of all and also relate their own efforts to the fulfillment of these needs.

148. Wherefore, we wish to honor appropriately those sons of ours who everywhere in the world, either by founding and fostering mutual-aid societies or some other type of association, watchfully strive that in all civic affairs farmers enjoy not merely economic prosperity but also a status in keeping with justice.

Vocation and Mission

149. Since everything that makes for man's dignity, perfection, and development seems to be invoked in agricultural labor, it is proper that man regard such work as an assignment from God with a sublime purpose. It is fitting, therefore, that man dedicate work of this kind to the most provident God who directs all events for the salvation of men. Finally, the farmer should take upon himself, in some measure, the task of educating himself and others for the advancement of civilization.

AID TO LESS DEVELOPED AREAS

150. It often happens that in one and the same country citizens enjoy different degrees of wealth and social advancement. This especially happens because they dwell in areas which, economically speaking, have grown at different rates. Where such is the case, justice and equity demand that the government make efforts either to remove or to minimize imbalances of this sort. Toward this end, efforts should be made, in areas where there has been less economic progress, to supply the principal public services, as indicated by circumstances of time and place and in accord with the general level of living. But in bringing this about, it is necessary to have very competent administration and organi-

zation to take careful account of the following: labor supply, internal migration, wages, taxes, interest rates, and investments in industries that foster other skills and developments—all of which will further not merely the useful employment of workers and the stimulation of initiative, but also the exploitation of resources locally available.

151. But it is precisely the measures for advancement of the general welfare which civil authorities must undertake. Hence, they should take steps, having regard for the needs of the whole community, that progress in agriculture, industry, and services be made at the same time and in a balanced manner so far as possible. They should have this goal in mind, that citizens in less developed countries—in giving attention to economic and social affairs, as well as to cultural matters—feel themselves to be the ones chiefly responsible for their own progress. For a citizen has a sense of his own dignity when he contributes the major share to progress in his own affairs.

152. Hence, those also who rely on their own resources and initiative should contribute as best they can to the equitable adjustment of economic life in their own community. Nay, more, those in authority should favor and help private enterprise in accordance with the *principle of subsidiarity,* in order to allow private citizens themselves to accomplish as much as is feasible.

IMBALANCES BETWEEN LAND AND POPULATION

153. It is appropriate to recall at this point that in a number of nations there exists a discrepancy between available agricultural land and the number of rural dwellers. Some nations experience a shortage of citizens, but have rich land resources; others have many citizens but an insufficiency of agricultural land.

154. Nor are there lacking nations wherein, despite their great resource potential, farmers use such primitive and obsolete methods of cultivation that they are unable to produce what is needed for the entire population. On the other hand, in certain countries, agriculture has so adapted itself to recent advances that farmers produce surpluses which to some extent harm the economy of the entire nation.

155. It is evident that both the solidarity of the human race and the sense of brotherhood which accords with Christian principles, require that some people lend others energetic help in many ways. Not merely would this result in a freer movement of goods, of capital, and of men, but it also would lessen imbalances between nations. We shall treat of this point in more detail below.

156. Here, however, we cannot fail to express our approval of the efforts of the Institute known as F.A.O. which concerns itself with the feeding of peoples and the improvement of agriculture. This Institute has the special goal of promoting mutual accord among peoples, of bringing it about that rural life is modernized in less developed nations, and finally, that help is brought to people experiencing food shortages.

REQUIREMENTS OF JUSTICE AS BETWEEN NATIONS DIFFERING ECONOMIC DEVELOPMENT
Problem of the Modern World

157. Perhaps the most pressing question of our day concerns the relationship between economically advanced commonwealths and those that are in process of development. The former enjoy the conveniences of life; the latter experience dire poverty. Yet, today men are so intimately associated in all parts of the world that they feel, as it were, as if they are members of one and the same household. Therefore, the nations that enjoy a sufficiency and abundance of everything may not overlook the plight of

other nations whose citizens experience such domestic problems that they are all but overcome by poverty and hunger, and are not able to enjoy basic human rights. This is all the more so, inasmuch as countries each day seem to become more dependent on each other. Consequently, it is not easy for them to keep the peace advantageously if excessive imbalances exist in their economic and social conditions.

158. Mindful of our role of universal father, we think it opportune to stress here what we have stated in another connection: "We all share responsibility for the fact that populations are undernourished.[40] (Therefore), it is necessary to arouse a sense of responsibility in individuals and generally, especially among those more blessed with this world's goods."[41]

159. As can be readily deduced, and as the Church has always seriously warned, it is proper that the duty of helping the poor and unfortunate should especially stir Catholics, since they are members of the Mystical Body of Christ. "In this we have come to know the love of God," said John the Apostle, "that He laid down His life for us; and we likewise ought to lay down our life for the brethren. He who has the goods of this world and sees his brother in need and closes his heart to him, how does the love of God abide in him?"[42]

160. Wherefore, we note with pleasure that countries with advanced productive systems are lending aid to less privileged countries, so that these latter may the more readily improve their condition.

Emergency Assistance

161. It is clear to everyone that some nations have surpluses in foodstuffs, particularly of farm products, while elsewhere large

---

40 *Allocution.* May 3, 1960; cf. A.A.S., LII (1960), p. 465.
41 Cf. *Ibid.*
42 1 John 3,16-17.

masses of people experience want and hunger. Now justice and humanity require that these richer countries come to the aid of those in need. Accordingly, to destroy entirely or to waste goods necessary for the lives of men, runs counter to our obligations in justice and humanity.

162. We are quite well aware that to produce surpluses, especially of farm products, in excess of the needs of a country, can occasion harm to various classes of citizens. Nevertheless, it does not therefore follow that nations with surpluses have no obligation to aid the poor and hungry where some particular emergency arises. Rather, diligent efforts should be made that inconveniences arising from surplus goods be minimized and borne by every citizen on a fair basis.

Scientific, Technical, and Financial Cooperation

163. However, the underlying causes of poverty and hunger will not be removed in a number of countries by these means alone. For the most part, the causes are to be found in the primitive state of the economy. To effect a remedy, all available avenues should be explored with a view, on the one hand, to instruct citizens fully in necessary skills and in carrying out their responsibilities, and, on the other hand, to enable them to acquire the means adapted to our times.

164. It has not escaped our attention that in recent years there has grown in many minds a deep awareness of their duty to aid poorer countries still lacking suitable economic development, in order that these may more readily make economic and social progress.

165. Toward this end, we look to councils, either of a number of nations, or within individual nations; we look to private enterprises and societies to exert daily more generous efforts on behalf of such countries, transmitting to them requisite produc-

tive skills. For the same reason help is given to as many youths as possible that they may study in the great universities of more developed countries, thus acquiring a knowledge of the arts and sciences in line with the standards of our time. Moreover, international banks, single nations, or private citizens often make loans to these countries that they may initiate various programs calculated to increase production. We gladly take this opportunity to give due praise to such generous activity. It is hoped that in the future the richer countries will make greater and greater efforts to provide developing countries with aid designed to promote sciences, technology, and economic life.

AVOIDANCE OF PAST ERRORS

166. In this matter we consider it our duty to offer some warnings.

167. First of all, it seems only prudent for nations which thus far have made little or no progress, to weigh well the principal factor in the advance of nations that enjoy abundance.

168. Prudent foresight and common need demand that not only more goods be produced, but that this be done more efficiently. Likewise, necessity and justice require that wealth produced be distributed equitably among all citizens of the commonwealth. Accordingly, efforts should be made to ensure that improved social conditions accompany economic advancement. And it is very important that such advances occur simultaneously in the agricultural, industrial, and various service sectors.

Respect for Individual Characteristics of Countries

169. It is indeed clear to all that countries in process of development often have their own individual characteristics, and that these arise from the nature of the locale, or from cultural tradition, or from some special trait of the citizens.

170. Now when economically developed countries assist the poorer ones, they not only should have regard for these characteristics and respect them, but also should take special care lest, in aiding these nations, they seek to impose their own way of life upon them.

Disinterested Aid

171. Moreover, economically developed countries should take particular care lest, in giving aid to poorer countries, they endeavor to turn the prevailing political situation to their own advantage, and seek to dominate them.

172. Should perchance such attempts be made, this clearly would be but another form of colonialism, which, although disguised in name, merely reflects their earlier but outdated dominion, now abandoned by many countries. When international relations are thus obstructed, the orderly progress of all peoples is endangered.

173. Genuine necessity, as well as justice, require that whenever countries give attention to the fostering of skills or commerce, they should aid the less developed nations without thought of domination, so that these latter eventually will be in a position to progress economically and socially on their own initiative.

174. If this be done, it will help much toward shaping a community of all nations, wherein each one, aware of its rights and duties, will have regard for the prosperity of all.

Respect for a Hierarchy of Values

175. There is no doubt that when a nation makes progress in science, technology, economic life, and the prosperity of its citizens, a great contribution is made to civilization. But all should realize that these things are not the highest goods, but only instruments for pursuing such goods.

9 *Social Doctrine*

176. Accordingly, we note with sorrow that in some nations economic life indeed progresses, but that not a few men are there to be found, who have no concern at all for the just ordering of goods. No doubt, these men either completely ignore spiritual values, or put these out of their minds, or else deny they exist. Nevertheless, while they pursue progress in science, technology, and economic life, they make so much of external benefits that for the most part they regard these as the highest goods of life. Accordingly, there are not lacking grave dangers in the help provided by more affluent nations for development of the poorer ones. For among the citizens of these latter nations, there is operative a general awareness of the higher values on which moral teaching rests—an awareness derived from ancient traditional custom which provides them with motivation.

177. Thus, those who seek to undermine in some measure the right instincts of these peoples, assuredly do something immoral. Rather, those attitudes, besides being held in honor, should be perfected and refined, since upon them true civilization depends.

Contribution of the Church

178. Moreover, the Church by divine right pertains to all nations. This is confirmed by the fact that she already is everywhere on earth and strives to embrace all peoples.

179. Now, those peoples whom the Church has joined to Christ have always reaped some benefits, whether in economic affairs or in social organization, as history and contemporary events clearly record. For everyone who professes Christianity promises and gives assurance that he will contribute as far as he can to the advancement of civil institutions. He must also strive with all his might not only that human dignity suffer no dishonor, but also, by the removal of every kind of obstacle, that all those forces be promoted which are conducive to moral living and contribute to it.

180. Moreover, when the Church infuses her energy into the life of a people, she neither is, nor feels herself to be, an alien institution imposed upon that people from without. This follows from the fact that wherever the Church is present, there individual men are reborn or resurrected in Christ. Those who are thus reborn or who have risen again in Christ feel themselves oppressed by no external force. Rather, realizing they have achieved perfect liberty, they freely move toward God. Hence, whatever is seen by them as good and morally right, that they approve and put into effect.

181. "The Church of Jesus Christ," as our predecessor Pius XII clearly stated, "is the faithful guardian of God's gracious wisdom. Hence, she makes no effort to discourage or belittle those characteristics and traits which are proper to particular nations, and which peoples religiously and tenaciously guard, quite justly, as a sacred heritage. She aims indeed at a unity which is profound and in conformity with that heavenly love whereby all are moved in their innermost being. She does not seek a uniformity which is merely external in its effects and calculated to weaken the fibre of the peoples concerned. And all careful rules that contribute to the wise development and growth within bounds of these capacities and forces, which indeed have their deeply rooted ethnic traits, have the Church's approval and maternal prayers, provided they are not in opposition to those duties which spring from the common origin and destiny of all mortal men." [43]

182. We note with deep satisfaction that Catholic men, citizens of the less developed nations, are for the most part second to no other citizens in furthering efforts of their countries to make progress economically and socially according to their capacity.

---

[43] Encyclical Letter *Summi Pontificatus;* A.A.S., XXXI (1939), p. 428-29.

183. Furthermore, we note that Catholic citizens of the richer nations are making extensive efforts to ensure that aid given by their own countries to needy countries is directed increasingly toward economic and social progress. In this connection, it seems specially praiseworthy that appreciable aid in various forms is provided increasingly each year to young people from Africa and Asia, so that they may pursue literary and professional studies in the great universities of Europe and America. The same applies to the great care that has been taken in training for every responsibility of their office men prepared to go to less developed areas, there to carry out their profession and duties.

184. To those sons of ours who, by promoting solicitously the progress of peoples and by spreading, as it were, a wholesome civilizing influence, everywhere demonstrate the perennial vitality of Holy Church and her effectiveness, we wish to express our paternal praise and gratitude.

POPULATION INCREASE AND ECONOMIC DEVELOPMENT

185. More recently, the question often is raised how economic organization and the means of subsistence can be balanced with population increase, whether in the world as a whole or within the needy nations.

Imbalance Between Population and Means of Subsistence

186. As regards the world as a whole, some, consequent to statistical reasoning, observe that within a matter of decades mankind will become very numerous, whereas economic growth will proceed much more slowly. From this some conclude that unless procreation is kept within limits, there subsequently will develop an even greater imbalance between the number of inhabitants and the necessities of life.

187. It is clearly evident from statistical records of less developed countries that, because recent advances in public health and in medicine are there widely diffused, the citizens have a longer life expectancy consequent to lowered rates of infant mortality. The birth rate, where it has traditionally been high, tends to remain at such levels, at least for the immediate future. Thus the birth rate in a given year exceeds the death rate. Meanwhile the productive systems in such countries do not expand as rapidly as the number of inhabitants. Hence, in poorer countries of this sort, the standard of living does not advance and may even deteriorate. Wherefore, lest a serious crisis occur, some are of the opinion that the conception or birth of humans should be avoided or curbed by every possible means.

The Terms of the Problem

188. Now to tell the truth, the interrelationship on a global scale between the number of births and available resources are such that we can infer grave difficulties in this matter do not arise at present, nor will in the immediate future. The arguments advanced in this connection are so inconclusive and controversial that nothing certain can be drawn from them.

189. Besides, God in His goodness and wisdom has, on the one hand provided nature with almost inexhaustible productive capacity; and, on the other hand, has endowed man with such ingenuity that, by using suitable means, he can apply nature's resources to the needs and requirements of existence. Accordingly, that the question posed may be clearly resolved, a course of action is not indeed to be followed whereby, contrary to the moral law laid down by God, procreative function also is violated. Rather, man should, by the use of his skills and science of every kind, acquire an intimate knowledge of the forces of nature and control them ever more extensively. Moreover, the advances hitherto made in science and technology give almost limitless promise for the future in this matter.

190. When it comes to questions of this kind, we are not unaware that in certain locales and also in poorer countries, it is often argued that in such an economic and social order, difficulties arise because citizens, each year more numerous, are unable to acquire sufficient food or sustenance where they live, and people do not show amicable cooperation to the extent they should.

191. But whatever be the situation, we clearly affirm these problems should be posed and resolved in such a way that man does not have recourse to methods and means contrary to his dignity, which are proposed by those persons who think of man and his life solely in material terms.

192. We judge that this question can be resolved only if economic and social advances preserve and augment the genuine welfare of individual citizens and of human society as a whole. Indeed, in a matter of this kind, first place must be accorded everything that pertains to the dignity of man as such, or to the life of individual men, than which nothing can be more precious. Moreover, in this matter, international cooperation is necessary, so that, conformably with the welfare of all, information, capital, and men themselves may move about among the peoples in orderly fashion.

Respect for the Laws of Life

193. In this connection, we strongly affirm that human life is transmitted and propagated through the instrumentality of the family which rests on marriage, one and indissoluble, and, so far as Christians are concerned, elevated to the dignity of a sacrament. Because the life of man is passed on to other men deliberately and knowingly, it therefore follows that this should be done in accord with the most sacred, permanent, inviolate prescriptions of God. Everyone without exception is bound to recognize and observe these laws. Wherefore, in this matter, no one is permitted

to use methods and procedures which may indeed be permissible to check the life of plants and animals.

194. Indeed, all must regard the life of man as sacred, since from its inception, it requires the action of God the Creator. Those who depart from this plan of God not only offend His divine majesty and dishonor themselves and the human race, but they also weaken the inner fibre of the commonwealth.

Education Toward a Sense of Responsibility

195. In these matters it is of great importance that new offspring, in addition to being very carefully educated in human culture and in religion—which indeed is the right and duty of parents—should also show themselves very conscious of their duties in every action of life. This is especially true when it is a question of establishing a family and of procreating and educating children. Such children should be imbued not only with a firm confidence in the providence of God, but also with a strong and ready will to bear the labors and inconveniences which cannot be lawfully avoided by anyone who undertakes the worthy and serious obligation of associating his own activity with God in transmitting life and in educating offspring. In this most important matter certainly nothing is more relevant than the teachings and supernatural aids provided by the Church. We refer to the Church whose right of freely carrying out her function must be recognized also in this connection.

Creation for Man's Benefit

106. When God, as we read in the book of Genesis, imparted human nature to our first parents, He assigned them two tasks, one of which complements the other. For He first directed: "Be fruitful and multiply," [44] and then immediately added: "Fill the earth and subdue it." [45]

---

44 Gen., 1, 28.
45 Ibid.

197. The second of these tasks, far from anticipating a destruction of goods, rather assigns them to the service of human life.

198. Accordingly, with great sadness we note two conflicting trends: on the one hand, the scarcity of goods is vaguely described as such that the life of men reportedly is in danger of perishing from misery and hunger; on the other hand, the recent discoveries of science, technical advances, and economic productivity are transformed into means whereby the human race is led toward ruin and a horrible death.

199. Now the provident God has bestowed upon humanity sufficient goods wherewith to bear with dignity the burdens associated with procreation of children. But this task will be difficult or even impossible if men, straying from the right road and with a perverse outlook, use the means mentioned above in a manner contrary to human reason or to their social nature, and hence, contrary to the directives of God Himself.

INTERNATIONAL COOPERATION

World Dimensions of Important Human Problems

200. Since the relationships between countries today are closer in every region of the world, by reason of science and technology, it is proper that peoples become more and more interdependent.

201. Accordingly, contemporary problems of moment—whether in the fields of science and technology, or of economic and social affairs, or of public administration, or of cultural advancement—these, because they may exceed the capacities of individual States, very often affect a number of nations and at times all the nations of the earth.

202. As a result, individual countries, although advanced in culture and civilization, in number and industry of citizens, in

wealth, in geographical extent, are not able by themselves to resolve satisfactorily their basic problems. Accordingly, because States must on occasion complement or perfect one another, they really consult their own interests only when they take into account at the same time the interests of others. Hence, dire necessity warns commonwealths to cooperate among themselves and provide mutual assistance.

Mutual Distrust

203. Although this becomes more and more evident each day to individuals and even to all peoples, men and especially those with high responsibility in public life, for the most part seem unable to accomplish the two things toward which peoples aspire. This does not happen because peoples lack scientific, technical, or economic means, but rather because they distrust one another. Indeed, men, and hence States, stand in fear of one another. One country fears lest another is contemplating aggression and lest the other seize an opportunity to put such plans into effect. Accordingly, countries customarily prepare defenses for their cities and homeland, namely, armaments designed to deter other countries from aggression.

204. Consequently, the energies of man and the resources of nature are very widely directed by peoples to destruction rather than to the advantage of the human family, and both individual men and entire peoples become so deeply solicitous that they are prevented from undertaking more important works.

Failure to Acknowledge the Moral Order

205. The cause of this state of affairs seems to be that men, more especially leaders of States, have differing philosophies of life. Some even dare to assert that there exists no law of truth and right which transcends external affairs and man himself, which of necessity pertains to everyone, and, finally, which is equitable for all men. Hence, men can agree fully and surely

about nothing, since one and the same law of justice is not accepted by all.

206. Although the word *justice* and the related term *demands of justice* are on everyone's lips, such verbalizations do not have the same meaning for all. Indeed, the opposite frequently is the case. Hence, when leaders invoke *justice* or the *demands of justice*, not only dc they disagree as to the meaning of the words, but frequently find in them an occasion of serious contention. And so they conclude that there is no way of achieving their rights or advantages, unless they resort to force, the root of very serious evils.

God, the Foundation of the Moral Order

207. That mutual faith may develop among rulers and nations and may abide more deeply in their minds, the laws of truth and justice first must be acknowledged and preserved on all sides.

208. However, the guiding principles of morality and virtue can be based only on God; apart from Him, they necessarily collapse. For man is composed not merely of body, but of soul as well, and is endowed with reason and freedom. Now such a composite being absolutely requires a moral law rooted in religion, which, far better than any external force or advantage, can contribute to the resolution of problems affecting the lives of individual citizens or groups of citizens, or with a bearing upon single States or all States together.

209. Yet, there are today those who assert that, in view of the flourishing state of science and technology, men can achieve the highest civilization even apart from God and by their own unaided powers. Nevertheless, it is because of this very progress in science and technology that men often find themselves involved in difficulties which affect all peoples, and which can be overcome only if they duly recognize the authority of God, author and ruler of man and of all nature.

210. That this is true, the advances of science seem to indicate, opening, up, as they do, almost limitless horizons. Thus, an opinion is implanted in many minds that inasmuch as mathematical sciences are unable to discern the innermost nature of things and their changes, or express them in suitable terms, they can scarcely draw inferences about them. And when terrified men see with their own eyes that the vast forces deriving from technology and machines can be used for destruction as well as for the advantage of peoples, they rightly conclude that things pertaining to the spirit and to moral life are to be preferred to all else, so that progress in science and technology, does not result in destruction of the human race, but prove useful as instruments of civilization.

211. Meanwhile it comes to pass that in more affluent countries men, less and less satisfied with external goods, put out of their minds the deceptive image of a happy life to be lived here forever. Likewise, not only do men grow daily more conscious that they are fully endowed with all the rights of the human person, but they also strive mightily that relations among themselves become more equitable and more conformed to human dignity. Consequently, men are beginning to recognize that their own capacities are limited, and they seek spiritual things more intensively than heretofore. All of which seems to give some promise that not only individuals, but even peoples may come to an understanding for extensive and extremely useful collaboration.

PART IV

RECONSTUCTION OF
SOCIAL RELATIONSHIPS
IN TRUTH, JUSTICE AND LOVE

Incomplete and Erroneous Philosophies of Life

212. As in the past, so too in our day, advances in science and technology have greatly multiplied relationships between citizens; it seems necessary, therefore, that the relationships themselves, whether within a single country or between all countries, be brought into more humane balance.

213. In this connection many systems of thought have been developed and committed to writing: some of these already have been dissipated as mist by the sun; other remain basically unchanged today; still others now elicit less and less response from men. The reason for this is that these popularized fancies neither encompass man, whole and entire, nor do they affect his inner being. Moreover, they fail to take into account the weaknesses of human nature, such as sickness and suffering: weaknesses that no economic or social system, no matter how advanced, can completely eliminate. Besides, men everywhere are moved by a profound and unconquerable sense of religion, which no force can ever destroy nor shrewdness suppress.

214. In our day, a very false opinion is popularized which holds that the sense of religion implanted in men by nature is to be regarded as something adventitious or imaginary, and hence, is to be rooted completely from the mind as altogether

inconsistent with the spirit of our age and the progress of civilization. Yet, this inward proclivity of man to religion confirms the fact that man himself was created by God, and irrevocably tends to Him. Thus we read in Augustine: "Thou hast made us for Thyself, O Lord, and our hearts are restless until they rest in Thee." [46]

215. Wherefore, whatever the progress in technology and economic life, there can be neither justice nor peace in the world, so long as men fail to realize how great is their dignity; for they have been created by God and are His children. We speak of God, who must be regarded as the first and final cause of all things He has created. Separated from God, man becomes monstrous to himself and others. Consequently, mutual relationships between men absolutely require a right ordering of the human conscience in relation to God, the source of all truth, justice, and love.

216. It is well known and recognized by everyone that in a number of countries, some of ancient Christian culture, many of our very dear brothers and sons have been savagely persecuted for a number of years. Now this situation, since it reveals the great dignity of the persecuted, and the refined cruelty of their persecutors, leads many to reflect on the matter, though it has not yet healed the wounds of the persecuted.

217. However, no folly seems more characteristic of our time than the desire to establish a firm and meaningful temporal order, but without God, its necessary foundation. Likewise, some wish to proclaim the greatness of man, but with the source dried up from which such greatness flows and receives nourishment: that is, by impeding and, if it were possible, stopping the yearn-

---

46 *Confessions*, I, 1.

ing of souls for God. But the turn of events in our times, whereby the hopes of many are shattered and not a few have come to grief, unquestionably confirm the words of Scripture: "Unless the Lord build the house, they labor in vain who built it." [47]

THE CHURCH'S TRADITIONAL TEACHING
REGARDING MAN'S SOCIAL LIFE

218. What the Catholic Church teaches and declares regarding the social life and relationships of men is beyond question for all time valid.

219. The cardinal point of this teaching is that individual men are necessarily the foundation, cause, and end of all social institutions. We are referring to human beings, insofar as they are social by nature, and raised to an order of existence that transcends and subdues nature.

220. Beginning with this very basic principle whereby the dignity of the human person is affirmed and defended, Holy Church—especially during the last century and with the assistance of learned priests and laymen, specialists in the field—has arrived at clear social teachings whereby the mutual relationships of men are ordered. Taking general norms into account, these principles are in accord with the nature of things and the changed conditions of man's social life, or with the special genius of our day. Moreover, these norms can be approved by all.

221. But today, more than ever, principles of this kind must not only be known and understood, but also applied to those systems and methods, which the various situations of time or place either suggest or require. This is indeed a difficult,

---

47 Ps. 126,1

though lofty, task. Toward its fulfillment we exhort not only our brothers and sons everywhere, but all men of good will.

Study of Social Matters

222. Above all, we affirm that the social teaching proclaimed by the Catholic Church cannot be separated from her traditional teaching regarding man's life.

223. Wherefore, it is our earnest wish that more and more attention be given to this branch of learning. First of all, we urge that attention be given to such studies in Catholic schools on all levels, and especially in seminaries, although we are not unaware that in some of these latter institutions this is already being done admirably. Moreover, we desire that social study of this sort be included among the religious materials used to instruct and inspire the lay apostolate, either in parishes or in associations. Let this diffusion of knowledge be accomplished by every modern means: that is, in journals, whether daily or periodical; in doctrinal books, both for the learned and the general reader; and finally, by means of radio and television.

224. We judge that our sons among the laity have much to contribute through their work and effort, that this teaching of the Catholic Church regarding the social question be more and more widely diffused. This they can do, not merely by learning it themselves and governing their actions accordingly, but also by taking special care that others also come to know its relevance.

225. Let them be fully persuaded that in no better way can they show this teaching to be correct and effective, than by demonstrating that present day social difficulties will yield to its application. In this way they will win minds today antagonistic to the teaching because they do not know it. Perhaps it will also happen that such men will find some enlightenment in the teaching.

APPLICATION OF SOCIAL TEACHING

226. But social norms of whatever kind are not only to be explained but also applied. This is especially true of the Church's teaching on social matters, which has truth as its guide, justice as its end, and love as its driving force.

227. We consider it, therefore, of the greatest importance that our sons, in addition to knowing these social norms, be reared according to them.

228. To be complete, the education of Christians must relate to the duties of every class. It is therefore necessary that Christians thus inspired conform their behavior in economic and social affairs to the teachings of the Church.

229. If it is indeed difficult to apply teaching of any sort to concrete situations, it is even more so when one tries to put into practice the teaching of the Catholic Church regarding social affairs. This is especially true for the following reasons; there is deeply rooted in each man an instinctive and immoderate love of his own interests; today there is widely diffused in society a materialistic philosophy of life; it is difficult at times to discern the demands of justice in a given situation.

230. Consequently, it is not enough for men to be instructed, according to the teachings of the Church, on their obligation to act in a Christian manner in economic and social affairs. They must also be shown ways in which they can properly fulfill their duty in this regard.

231. We do not regard such instructions as sufficient, unless there be added to the work of instruction that of the formation of man, and unless some action follow upon the teaching, by way of experience.

232. Just as, proverbially, no one really enjoys liberty unless

he uses it, so no one really knows how to act according to Catholic teaching in the economic and social fields, unless he acts according to this teaching in the same area.

A Task for Lay Apostolate

233. Accordingly, in popular instruction of this kind, it seems proper that considerable attention be paid to groups promoting the lay apostolate, especially those whose aim is to ensure that efforts in our present concern draw their inspiration wholly from Christian law. Seeing that members of such groups can first train themselves by daily practice in these matters, they subsequently will be able the better to instruct young people in fulfilling obligations of this kind.

234. It is not inappropriate in this connection to remind all, the great no less than the lowly, that the will to preserve moderation and to bear difficulties, by God's grace, can in no wise be separated from the meaning of life handed down to us by Christian wisdom.

235. But today, unfortunately, very many souls are preoccupied with an inordinate desire for pleasure. Such persons see nothing more important in the whole of life than to seek pleasure, to quench the thirst for pleasure. Beyond doubt, grave ills to both soul and body proceed therefrom. Now in this matter, it must be admitted that one who judges even with the aid of human nature alone, concludes that it is the part of the wise and prudent man to preserve balance and moderation in everything, and to restrain the lower appetites. He who judges matters in the light of divine revelation, assuredly will not overlook the fact that the Gospel of Christ and the Catholic Church, as well as the ascetical tradition handed down to us, all demand that Christians steadfastly mortify themselves and bear the inconveniences of life with singular patience. These virtues, in addition to fostering a firm and moderate rule of mind over body, also present an oppor-

tunity of satisfying the punishment due to sin, from which, except for Jesus Christ and His Immaculate Mother, no one is exempt.

PRACTICAL SUGGESTIONS

236. The teachings in regard to social matters for the most part are put into effect in the following three stages: first, the actual situation is examined; then, the situation is evaluated carefully in relation to these teachings; then only is it decided what can and should be done in order that the traditional norms may be adapted to circumstances of time and place. These three steps are at times expressed by the three words: *observe, judge, act.*

237. Hence, it seems particularly fitting that youth not merely reflect upon this order of procedure, but also, in the present connection, follow it to the extent feasible, lest what they have learned be regarded merely as something to be thought about but not acted upon.

238. However, when it comes to reducing these teachings to action, it sometimes happens that even sincere Catholic men have differing views. When this occurs they should take care to have and to show mutual esteem and regard, and to explore the extent to which they can work in cooperation among themselves. Thus they can in good time accomplish what necessity requires. Let them also take great care not to weaken their efforts in constant controversies. Nor should they, under pretext of seeking what they think best, meanwhile, fail to do what they can and hence should do.

239. But in the exercise of economic and social functions, Catholics often come in contact with men who do not share their view of life. On such occasions, those who profess Catholicism must take special care to be consistent and not compromise in

matters wherein the integrity of religion or morals would suffer harm. Likewise, in their conduct they should weigh the opinions of others with fitting courtesy and not measure everything in the light of their own interests. They should be prepared to join sincerely in doing whatever is naturally good or conducive to good. If, indeed, it happens that in these matters sacred authorities have prescribed or decreed anything, it is evident that this judgment is to be obeyed promptly by Catholics. For it is the Church's right and duty not only to safeguard principles relating to the integrity of religion and morals, but also to pronounce authoritatively when it is a matter of putting these principles into effect.

Manifold Action and Responsibility

240. But what we have said about the norms of instruction should indeed be put into practice. This has special relevance for those beloved sons of ours who are in the ranks of the laity inasmuch as their activity ordinarily centers around temporal affairs and making plans for the same.

241. To carry out this noble task, it is necessary that laymen not only should be qualified, each in his own profession, and direct their energies in accordance with rules suited to the objective aimed at, but also should conform their activity to the teachings and norms of the Church in social matters. Let them put sincere trust in her wisdom; let them accept her admonitions as sons. Let them reflect that, when in the conduct of life they do not carefully observe principles and norms laid down by the Church in social matters, and which we ourselves reaffirm, then they are negligent in their duty and often injure the rights of others. At times, matters can come to a point where confidence in this teaching is diminished, as if it were indeed excellent but really lacks the force which the conduct of life requires.

A Grave Danger

242. As we have already noted, in this present age men have searched widely and deeply into the laws of nature. Then they invented instruments whereby they can control the forces of nature; they have perfected and continue to perfect remarkable works worthy of deep admiration. Nevertheless, while they endeavor to master and transform the external world, they are also in danger, lest they become neglectful and weaken the powers of body and mind. This is what our predecessor of happy memory, Pius XI, noted with sorrow of spirit in his Encyclical Letter *Quadragesimo Anno*: "And so bodily labor, which was decreed by divine providence for the good of man's body and soul even after original sin, has too often been changed into an instrument of perversion: for dead matter leaves the factory ennobled and transformed whereas men are there corrupted and degraded." [48]

243. And our predecessor of happy memory, Pius XII, rightly asserted that our age is distinguished from others precisely by the fact that science and technology have made incalculable progress, while men themselves have departed correspondingly from a sense of dignity. It is a "monstrous masterpiece" of this age "to have transformed man, as it were, into a giant as regards the order of nature, yet in the order of the supernatural and the enternal, to have changed him into a pygmy." [49]

244. Too often in our day is verified the testimony of the Psalmist concerning worshipers of false gods, namely human beings in their activity very frequently neglect themselves, but admire their own works as if these were gods: "Their idols are silver and gold; the handiwork of men." [50]

---

48 *Acta Apostolicae Sedis*, XXIII (1931), p. 221f.
49 Radio Broadcast, Christmas Eve, 1953; cf. A.A.S., XLVI (1954), p. 10.
50 Ps. 113, 4.

Respect for the Hierarchy of Values

245. Wherefore, aroused by the pastoral zeal wherewith we embrace all men, we strongly urge our sons that, in fulfilling their duties and in pursuing their goals, they do not allow their consciousness of responsibilities to grow cool, nor neglect the order of the more important goods.

246. For it is indeed clear that the Church has always taught and continues to teach that advances in science and technology and the prosperity resulting therefrom, are truly to be counted as good things and regarded as signs of the progress of civilization. But the Church likewise teaches that goods of this kind are to be judged properly in accordance with their natures: they are always to be considered as instruments for man's use, the better to achieve his highest end: that he can the more easily improve himself, in both the natural and supernatural orders.

247. Wherefore, we ardently desire that our sons should at all times heed the words of the divine Master: "For what does it profit a man, if he gain the whole world, but suffer the loss of his own soul? Or what will a man give in exchange for his soul?" [51]

Sanctification of Holy Days

248. Not unrelated to the above admonitions is the one having to do with rest to be taken on feast days.

249. In order that the Church may defend the dignity with which man is endowed, because he is created by God and because God has breathed into him a soul to His own image, she has never failed to insist that the third commandment: "Remember to keep holy the Sabbath day," [52] be carefully observed by all.

---

51 Matt. 16, 26.
52 Exod. 20, 8.

It is the right of God, and within His power, to order that man put aside a day each week for proper and due worship of the divinity. He should direct his mind to heavenly things, setting aside daily business. He should explore the depths of his conscience in order to know how necessary and inviolable are his relations with God.

250. In addition, it is right and necessary for man to cease for a time from labor, not merely to relax his body from daily hard work and likewise to refresh himself with decent recreation, but also to foster family unity, for this requires that all its members preserve a community of life and peaceful harmony.

251. Accordingly, religion, moral teaching, and care of health in turn require that relaxation be had at regular times. The Catholic Church has decreed for many centuries that Christians observe this day of rest on Sunday, that they be present on the same day at the Eucharistic Sacrifice because it renews the memory of the divine Redemption and at the same time imparts its fruits to the souls of men.

252. But we note with deep sorrow, and we cannot but reprove the many who, though they perhaps do not deliberately despise this holy law, yet more and more frequently disregard it. Whence it is that our very dear workingmen almost necessarily suffer harm, both as to the salvation of their souls and to the health of their bodies.

253. And so, taking into account the needs of soul and body, we exhort, as it were, with the words of God Himself, all men, whether public officials or representatives of management and labor, that they observe this command of God Himself and of the Catholic Church, and judge in their souls that they have a responsibility to God and society in this regard.

RENEWED DEDICATION

254. From what we have briefly touched upon above, let none of our sons conclude, and especially the laity, that they act prudently if, in regard to the transitory affairs of this life, they become quite remiss in their specific Christian contributions. On the contrary, we reaffirm that they should be daily more zealous in carrying out this role.

255. Indeed, when Christ our Lord made that solemn prayer for the unity of His Church, He asked this from the Father on behalf of His disciples: "I do not pray that Thou take them out of the world, but that Thou keep them from evil." [53] Let no one imagine that there is any opposition between these two things so that they cannot be properly reconciled: namely, the perfection of one's own soul and the business of this life, as if one had no chance but to abandon the activities of this world in order to strive for Christian perfection, or as if one could not attend to these pursuits without endangering his own dignity as a man and as a Christian.

256. However, it is in full accord with the designs of God's providence that men develop and perfect themselves by exercise of their daily tasks, for this is the lot of practically everyone in the affairs of this mortal life. Accordingly, the role of the Church in our day is very difficult: to reconcile man's modern respect for progress with the norms of humanity and of the Gospel teaching. Yet, the times call the Church to this role; indeed, we may say, earnestly beseech her, not merely to pursue the higher goals, but also to safeguard her accomplishments without harm to herself. To achieve this, as we have already said, the Church especially asks the cooperation of the laity. For this reason, in their dealings with men, they are bound to exert effort in such a

---

53 John 17, 15.

way that while fulfilling their duties to others, they do so in union with God through Christ, for the increase of God's glory. Thus the Apostle Paul asserts: "Whether you eat or drink, or do anything else, do all for the glory of God." [54] And elsewhere: "Whatever you do in word or in work, do all in the name of the Lord Jesus Christ, giving thanks to God the Father through Him." [55]

Greater Effectiveness in Temporal Affairs

257. As often, therefore, as human activity and institutions having to do with the affairs of this life, help toward spiritual perfection and everlasting beatitude, the more they are to be regarded as an efficacious way of obtaining the immediate end to which they are directed by their very nature. Thus, valid for all time is that noteworthy sentence of the divine Master: "Seek first the kingdom of God and His justice, and all these things shall be given you besides." [56] For he who is, as it were, a *light in the Lord,* [57] and walks as a *son of light,* [58] he perceives more clearly what the requirements of justice are, in the various sectors of human zeal, even in those that involve greater difficulties because of the excessive love which many have for their own interests, or those of their country, or race. It must be added that when one is motivated by Christian charity, he cannot but love others, and regard the needs, sufferings and joys of others as his own. His work, wherever it be, is constant, adaptable, humane, and has concern for the needs of others: For "Charity is patient, is kind; charity does not envy, is not pretentious, is not puffed up, is not ambitious, is not self seeking, is not provoked; thinks no evil, does not rejoice over wickedness, but rejoices with the

---

54 I Cor. 10, 31.
55 Col. 3, 17.
56 Matt. 6, 33.
57 Eph. 5, 8.
58 Cf. *Ibid.*

truth; bears with all things, believes all things, hopes all things, endures all things." [59]

LIVING MEMBERS OF THE MYSTICAL BODY OF CHRIST

258. But we do not wish to bring this letter of ours to a close, Venerable Brothers, without recalling to your minds that most fundamental and true element of Catholic teaching, whereby we learn that we are living members of His Mystical Body, which is the Church: "For as the body is one and has many members, and all the members of the body, many as they are, form one body, so also is it with Christ." [60]

259. Wherefore, we urgently exhort all our sons in every part of the world, whether clergy or laity, that they fully understand how great is the nobility and dignity they derive from being joined to Christ, as branches to the vine, as He Himself said: "I am the vine, you are the branches," [61] and that they are sharers of His divine life. Whence it is, that if Christians are also joined in mind and heart with the most Holy Redeemer, when they apply themselves to temporal affairs, their work in a way is a continuation of the labor of Jesus Christ Himself, drawing from it strength and redemptive power: "He who abides in Me, and I in him, he bears much fruit." [62] Human labor of this kind is so exalted and ennobled that it leads men engaged in it to spiritual perfection, and can likewise contribute to the diffusion and propagation of the fruits of the Redemption to others. So also it results in the flow of that Gospel leaven, as it were, through the veins of civil society wherein we live and work.

---

59 I Cor. 13, 4-7.
60 I Cor., 12, 12.
61 John 15, 5.
62 *Ibid.*

260. Although it must be admitted that the times in which we live are torn by increasingly serious errors, and are troubled by violent disturbances, yet, it happens that the Church's laborers in this age of ours have access to enormous fields of apostolic endeavor. This inspires us with uncommon hope.

261. Venerable Brothers and beloved sons, beginning with that marvelous letter of Leo, we have thus far considered with you the varied and serious issues which pertain to the social conditions of our time. From them we have drawn norms and teachings, upon which we especially exhort you not merely to meditate deeply, but also to do what you can to put them into effect. If each one of you does his best courageously, it will necessarily help in no small measure to establish the kingdom of Christ on earth. This is indeed: "A kingdom of justice, of love and of peace." [63] And this we shall some day leave to go to that heavenly beatitude, for which we were made by God, and which we ask for with most ardent prayers.

262. For it is a question here of the teaching of the Catholic and Apostolic Church, mother and teacher of all nations, whose light illumines, sets on fire, inflames. Her warning voice, filled with heavenly wisdom, reaches out to every age. Her power always provides efficacious and appropriate remedies for the growing needs of men, for the cares and solicitudes of this mortal life. With this voice, the age-old song of the Psalmist is in marvelous accord, to strengthen at all times and to uplift our souls: "I will hear what God proclaims; the Lord—for He proclaims peace to His people, and to His faithful ones, and to those who put in Him their hope. Near indeed is His salvation to those who fear Him, glory dwelling in our land. Kindness and truth shall meet; justice and peace shall kiss. Truth shall spring out of the earth, and justice shall look down from heaven. The Lord Himself will

---

63 *Preface of Jesus Christ the King.*

give His benefits; our land shall yield its increase. Justice shall walk before Him, and salvation, along the way of His steps." [64]

263. This is the plea, Venerable Brothers, we make at the close of this Letter, to which we have for a considerable time directed our concern about the Universal Church. We desire that the divine Redeemer of mankind, "who has become for us God-given wisdom, and justice, and sanctification, and redemption" [65] may reign and triumph gloriously in all things and over all things, for centuries on end. We desire that, in a properly organized order of social affairs, all nations will at last enjoy prosperity, and happiness, and peace.

264. As an evidence of these wishes, and a pledge of our paternal good will, we affectionately bestow in the Lord our apostolic blessing upon you, Venerable Brothers, and upon all the faithful committed to your care, and especially upon those who will reply with generosity to our appeals.

265. Given at Rome, at Saint Peter's, the fifteenth day of May, in the year 1961, the third year of our Pontificate.

JOHN XXIII, POPE

Index

Bibliography

The Functional Economy by Bernard William Dempsey, published by Prentice Hall.

Communism and Christianity by Martin D'Arcy, published by Penguin (1956).

Policy for the West by Barbara Ward, Penguin.

Christian Humanism by Louis Bouyer, published by Geoffrey Chapman.

The Springs of Morality A Catholic Symposium, Edited by John M. Todd, published by Burns & Oates.

Marxism Past and Present by R.N. Carew Hunt, published by Geoffrey Bles.

The Theory and Practice of Communism by R.N. Carew Hunt, published by Geoffrey Bles.

God, Man and the Universe—A Christian Answer to Modern Materialism A selection of essays, edited by Jacques de Bivort la Saudee, published by Burns & Oates.

A Map of Life by F. J. Sheed, published by Sheed & Ward.

Economic Control by Michael Fogarty, published by Routledge & Keegan Paul.

Church and State by L. Sturzo, published by Geoffrey Bles.

Code of Social Principles 3rd. Ed. English translantion, published by Catholic Social Guild, 1952.

Communism and Man, F.J. Sheed, published by Sheed & Ward.

Welfare and Taxation, Colin Clark, published by Catholic Social Guild, 1954.

The Whole Man Goes to Work, by Henry L. Nunn, published by Harper & Brothers (New York).

Philosophy of Value by Leo R. Ward, Burns Oates & Washbourne.

———

The translation of Quadragesimo Anno and Rerum Novarum used throughout was taken from the "Social Order" and "The Workers' Charter" published jointly by the Catholic Truth Society and The Catholic Social Guild, Oxford. The translation of the great Christmas Message of Pope Pius XII of 1942 is that of Canon George Smith published also by the Catholic Truth Society. The translation of the Encyclical "Mater et Magistra" is that of William J. Gibbons, S. J., published by the Paulist Press, 180 Varick St. New York 14, N.Y.